THE ART OF SHOOTING

CHARLES LANCASTER

HELLIS, BEESLEY & WATSON

GUNMAKERS

LONDON

FOURTEENTH EDITION

1985

ASHFORD PRESS PUBLISHING

Published by ASHFORD PRESS PUBLISHING 1985
1 Church Road, Shedfield, Hants. SO3 2HW

First Published	...	...	...	...	...	1889
Second Edition	...	...	...	...	...	1889
Third Edition ...	...	...	...	...	...	1891
Fourth Edition	...	...	...	...	...	1892
Fifth Edition ...	...	...	...	...	...	1894
Sixth Edition ...	...	...	...	...	...	1898
Seventh Edition	...	...	...	...	...	1906
Eighth Edition	...	...	...	...	...	1924
Ninth Edition ...	...	...	...	...	...	1937
Tenth Edition	...	...	...	...	...	1942
Reprinted	...	...	...	...	...	1943
Eleventh Edition	...	...	...	...	...	1945
Reprinted	...	...	...	...	...	1946
Twelfth Edition	...	...	...	...	...	1954
Thirteenth Edition	...	...	...	...	...	1962

British Library Cataloguing in Publication Data

Lancaster, Charles
    The art of shooting.   14th ed.
    1. Hunting   Great Britain
    2. Title
    799.2'13   SK185

    ISBN 0-907069-11-8

Printed and bound in Great Britain by
Biddles Ltd, Guildford and King's Lynn

PREFACE TO THE FOURTEENTH EDITION.

> ". . . . nobody shoots so well but what they might
> shoot better."
> G. Teasdale – Buckell (Experts on
> Guns and Shooting, 1900).

Despite miracle advances in technology – surprisingly, except for the replacement of Damascus with fine quality steel barrels – the double-barrelled shotgun, as developed more than a hundred years ago, is still substantially unchanged.

More surprisingly a book written by a prominent gun-maker of that classic period is still regarded, nearly a century later, as *the* finest work on the art of shooting.

The author Charles Lancaster* besides having been a prolific inventor in the 'mystery' of gunmaking, as it was anciently called, also enjoyed, in the phrase of a critic reviewing the first edition of *The Art of Shooting* (1889), ". . . . the reputation of being an excellent coach."

Above all Charles Lancaster was a visionary – his unique illustrative method of coaching the chair-bound shooter so that he could clearly imagine himself holding the gun and being 'stood behind' in the shooting field was inspiringly original. All Lancaster's views on how to carry a gun for greater efficiency and comfort, involving the subtleties of handgrip, body posture and barrel direction; all his views on how to make clean kills with crossing, approaching, departing, ascending or descending targets were initially captured by the camera – before an artist was commissioned to illustrate the book.

From these photographs James Temple was instructed to make some fifty drawings so as to 'bring out' those points which not only more effectively illustrate the first principles of shooting at moving objects but graphically convey most of what is known of the discipline of safety when shooting in company.

The drawings, complemented by Lancaster's terse but well written text, have made *The Art of Shooting*, for those learning to shoot, the best primer extant. For the experienced shots who are dissatisfied with their performance and for those who shoot badly ". . . . for want of some judicious instruction from a master of the craft" it is a godsend. For the rest, as one American correspondent cogently pointed out ". . . . no intelligent sportsman will regret the time or money it has cost him."

*The author of the book was H.A.A. Thorn who purchased Charles Lancaster's business, including the right to his name, in 1878. Thorn was the first man to claim that he could see shot in the air.

March 1985   FRED BULLER

The preface of the ninth edition expresses so well the intentions and hopes of the author and his successors that even after forty eight years it is repeated without apology.

PREFACE TO NINTH EDITION.

A great deal of water has flowed under London Bridge since Charles Lancaster wrote his treatise on the Art of Shooting in 1889. Since that date controversy on many points connected with guns and ammunition has waxed and waned, blazed up afresh and finally fizzled out to become History just as it has done on other subjects and will no doubt continue to do. Time has a mellowing influence as well as a wasting hand and opposing dogmatic opinions are eventually accorded their proper places by Posterity.

On first reading the book many years ago, the present writer's strongest impression was one of amazement that Mr. Lancaster in the multitudinous duties incidental to the carrying on of a gunmaking business could have found time to master and set out all the details he has so lucidly expressed. Quite obviously he must have deprived himself of his leisure and burned much midnight oil in his zeal to place his knowledge of shooting so freely at the service of sportsmen. In our opinion the great success and continued popularity of " The Art of Shooting" has been largely due to the Author's simplicity of description and avoidance of too much technical matter, which as a rule is so interesting to the few and so boring to the many.

Generally speaking, in the last half-century there has been a gradual tendency to use guns for ordinary game shooting with somewhat shorter barrels, with less choke, of lighter weight and loaded with a slightly smaller charge of shot. While all this has enhanced the pleasure of shooting, it has been accomplished without any perceptible loss of efficiency.

In arranging to publish a ninth edition it was obvious that if due allowance was made for these and other improvements about which no possible difference of opinion could exist, the book as a whole could hardly be improved upon. Although many changes in the methods of shooting have taken place since " villainous saltpetre " was first used for sporting purposes, very few of these have been since the first edition was published. That being so, the greater part of the information then given is equally suitable to-day, while the remainder has been brought up to date in accordance with present developments.

There was no difficulty in deciding to retain the original illustrations and those who derive amusement from them need hardly be reminded that Dame Fashion is a fickle, fast-moving jade, with whom it is extremely difficult to keep pace. Solomon declared there was no new thing under the sun and History is said to repeat itself, so who knows but what the children or grandchildren of the present generation may be seen wearing whiskers and deer-stalkers or top hats when they sally forth to attempt to put salt on the tails of the various delightful game birds and animals that abound in these islands.

Whether the reader is a beginner or an experienced shot and whether (all else being equal) his idea of a " crowded hour of glorious life " is shooting on the grand scale or getting " far from the madding crowd's ignoble strife " to potter on a remote rough shoot with a boon companion and a favourite dog, he will, we trust, still derive much pleasure and obtain many useful hints from a study of Charles Lancaster's world-famous book, " The Art of Shooting."

W.R.H. ROBSON

1937.

CONTENTS

PART I.

PART II.

CONTENTS—*continued.*

Acknowledgement is gratefully made to Imperial Metal Industries Ltd., for their courtesy in allowing the reproduction of many of the Tables given in Part II.

A FATHER'S ADVICE TO HIS SON.

If a sportsman true you'd be, listen carefully to me :—

Never, never, let your gun
Pointed be at anyone :
That it may unloaded be
Matters not the least to me.

When a hedge or fence you cross,
Though of time it cause a loss,
From your gun the cartridge take
For the greater safety's sake.

If 'twixt you and neighbouring gun
Bird may fly or beast may run,
Let this maxim e'er be thine :
' Follow not across the line.'

Stops and beaters, oft unseen,
Lurk behind some leafy screen :
Calm and steady always be—
' Never shoot where you can't see.'

Keep your place and silent be ;
Game can hear and game can see.
Don't be greedy. Better spared
Is a pheasant than one shared.

You may kill or you may miss,
But at all times think of this—
' All the pheasants ever bred
Won't repay for one man dead.'

MARK BEAUFOY.

Reproduced by kind permission of Mrs. Gwendolyn Beaufoy.

THE ART OF SHOOTING

PART I

A WORD OF ADVICE.

THE first lesson to be learnt by the beginner, and one to be remembered all his life, is " Safety."

Always look upon a gun as a death-dealing weapon. Therefore, at all times, be careful in which direction it is pointed, so as to avoid any possibility of its being in line or " laid on " to any person or thing you would wish not to hit (*see* pages 47 and 48).

Do not forget this when you are doing something apart from actual shooting; for example, when picking up a bird.

Accidents easily happen; therefore, whether loaded or unloaded, always exercise the greatest amount of caution in the handling of gun, rifle, pistol or revolver.

No. 1]

Missing by "skying" with a stock too long and straight.

The above simple words are easily remembered, and there can be no excuse whatever in the mere saying, "I did not know it was loaded," after mischief has been done. Truly, "the loaded gun has slain its thousands, and the unloaded one its tens of thousands."

I once read the last words of a suicide, in which he stated he hoped the jury would not return a verdict of "accidental death" or "death by misadventure," because he thoroughly understood what he was doing at the time he shot himself, and did not wish it handed down to posterity that he belonged to the class of idiots who inadvertently, would handle a weapon in such a way as to cause risk to themselves or others.

THE FIT OF A GUN.

A good fit in a gun is as necessary for a successful shot as a well-fitting shoe is for a pedestrian. Some men are smaller than others, and a man must have his gun to fit him the same as his clothes; consequently the gun that fits one may not fit another. Men's likes and dislikes, too, are as different as their faces, and what suits one will not suit another.

To test if a gun is really a fit, pin a piece of white paper on a wall or a tree, then put the gun up at it quickly, with both eyes open, and after several such trials one can tell how the gun suits. If it mounts too high, the stock is too straight (*see* page 10)—if low, the stock is too bent; if to the left, it should be cast-off to the right—if to the right, cast off should be reduced; if the stock catches in bringing it up on the object, it is too long and wants shortening. To ascertain the latter, by leaning forward from the hips, a gun that is too long can be mounted to its proper place and, by gradually returning to the upright position until the gun catches, the excess of length may be demonstrated. A tall man will require more bend and length than a shorter one; and a stout man will require more cast-off than a thin one.

In selecting a gun the buyer must at all times bear in mind that there is a handicap in weight and bore of guns, as in all sports where fatigue and accuracy come in; therefore one man can use a gun at $6\frac{1}{2}$ or 7 lbs., whereas another can only carry, say, 6 lbs. Although in 12 bores modern design has done much to reduce the effects, faster recoil necessarily occurs with a light gun than with a heavy one firing the same cartridges ; it is better therefore to use a smaller load, or a gun of smaller bore, than to shoot with a gun that is likely to tell its tale against you in excessive recoil, because no one can shoot even moderately well if he is getting punished.

Some of the matters here briefly touched upon will be dealt with more fully in subsequent pages, but it should now be urged that your gunmaker is the proper person to advise as to the most suitable type of gun for you. Although the fore-going rules as to stock measurements are basic, you cannot expect to apply them with the accuracy of the experienced fitter, in whose hands the " try-gun " can be adjusted until the length, bend and cast are absolutely right for you.

THE ADJUSTABLE " TRY-GUN "

Carrying for a long walk.

CARRYING AND LOADING A GUN.

I consider it half the battle, where a gun has to be carried all day, over good or bad ground, to understand the easiest method of doing so without undue fatigue. Therefore I submit the illustrations (Nos. 2 and 3) as being likely to convey the idea without a long wordy description; but I prefer the manner so well shown in illustration No. 3, page 16—where the gun is being carried on the right shoulder and hand—because it admits of the gun being brought to cover an object immediately without changing the hold or grasp of the stock. This, however, should not be done in rain, otherwise water will run down the barrels, through the striker holes and into the locks.

But please note that barrels may be dented and damaged when two sportsmen are walking side by side (*see* page 17); then it is better to let the gun rest on the arm, either shut or open, the latter a convenient and obviously safe way.

The position for loading a gun, or placing it to "safe"* should be studied carefully—not only with a view to ease in loading, but more especially so that, when in the act of opening the gun to reload

* A hammerless ejector is always at " full cock " when it has been closed after opening, and remains so until it is fired, irrespective of the position of the " safety " thumb piece, which locks the triggers only.

Carrying, yet ready

Barrels are often dented and damaged when two sportsmen are walking
side by side; then it is better to let the gun rest on the arm, either shut
or open, the latter a convenient and obviously safe way.

No. 4]

[17

2

No. 5]   Convenient holding for loading.   [18

(*see* page 18) after having only fired one barrel, or in closing the gun when reloaded (*see* page 20), the barrels may never by any chance be allowed to cover or point near dog or man. This I wish especially to impress upon everyone's mind, whether beginner or not, because I have noticed it frequently occur. Should the gun go off by accident, when it is pointing in a clear direction little harm can be done ; whereas, if carelessly pointed, a sad loss of limb or life may take place.

In addition to unloading at the end of a drive or when negotiating a fence, it is most necessary to look through the barrels to make sure they are free from any obstruction before starting a day's shooting and before you reload after crossing a fence or putting the gun down anywhere.

At lunch time and other pauses, stand the gun in a safe place where it will not be knocked over by a dog. If it is raining, the muzzles should be down, so that water will run off, instead of into the mechanism, but avoid the possibility of mud entering the nose-ends.

The verses printed on page viii should certainly be known by heart, but it is even more important to understand the rules embodied and to carry them into practice.

Closing the wrong way, the cartridges falling out.

[20

Closing the gun by the toe of the stock, a safe way for "Loaders" and "Guns."

No. 6]

HANDLING AND POSITION.

At all times it is best, and most essential, to get a firm hold of the gun with both hands ; but care must be taken to notice that, as the left hand has generally to come over to the right side for a correct alignment, you should not hold the barrels too far forward, or the left hand will not come over, and will tend to check the gun from taking a true and square shot, especially so on the right. It is also very important to prevent the fingers of the left hand from " crossing the right barrel " and resting on the top rib. When taking a shot be careful that you have both feet well placed, the left foot slightly in advance of the right, but in an easy position ; the body bending forward so that the chin plumbs the left foot—the knees never bent and the weight of the body on the left foot, the heel of the right slightly raised.

Should a bird go to right or left, be careful to make a complete change of front, *i.e.*, half-turn to the side required ; and always be careful to use the right foot as the pivot, moving only the left from the ground— turning on the right by moving the body to the direction of the flight of the bird. This allows the body to be square to it, and prevents an unpleasant recoil on the arm, or perhaps a kick on the face, which

Extracting cartridges before getting over a fence.

N.B.—This should always be done.

may be felt for the next few shots and cause the shooter to flinch.

Never draw back the right foot as it destroys the aim and is very prejudicial to the shooting position. In taking up your position for a drive always find a firm footing—for choice, the left foot should be lower than the right, as it will naturally tend to throw the body forward. The body being forward (*see* page 28) allows the gun to be mounted cleanly without fear of catching, gives greater resistance for the recoil of the first barrel and the body will then be in an upright position for the second ; but if the first barrel is fired with the body erect, the recoil will tend to throw the body out of balance, and this takes time to correct. The loss of a second means that the bird may have travelled 15 or 20 yards, thereby preventing the chance of a second shot at a reasonable distance.

I.—Walk with barrels well up, and lying towards the left.

II.—Walking ceased. Barrels thrown over to the right side ready to be

III.—Weight of body thrown on left foot, and gun brought smartly to

ELEMENTARY PRACTICE.

" Practice makes perfect " is an old and true adage ; and in shooting, as in all other sports where ease of movement combined with well-hardened sinews and muscles are requisite, those who practise most will become proficient first. I advise the handling of a gun once or twice a week all the year round, if even for only ten minutes at a time ; but oftener than this is necessary for a beginner.

Not many people have the chance of as much shooting as they would like, so it is essential to keep practising until you have confidence in your handling. Valuable shooting days will then not be wasted by having no proper foundation upon which to build experience in the field.

With a view to assisting the beginner (and others) to overcome the flurry when game rises, and the consequent careless bringing of the gun to the shoulder, whereby the degree of exactness with which it should be done is spoilt, I insert illustrations (No. 8), arranged numerically, to show the order in which these position exercises should be made, and so admit of a good view of the object to be shot. I hope they will be useful in assisting my readers to overcome

No 9]   Bad positions—to be avoided.   [26

the faults mentioned and that whereas previously birds have been missed with both barrels, subsequently a right and left will be easily taken with the coolness exhibited by a first-class shot.

When you have a gun, don't forget where it is, but keep it in some handy, get-at-able place. Many who really feel inclined to practise often do not do so because "it's too much bother to get it from the gun-case,"—whereas, if it is always kept within reach and sight, there is no excuse to be made, and the work is done.

To the beginner I say, be most careful how you commence, so as not to get into a bad position (*see* page 26), because that makes the work much more difficult and very tiring. Take the gun in both hands, the right held well round the hand of the stock with the middle finger firmly against the back of the guard or well clear of it, otherwise there will be bruising. If the fault cannot be cured, the effects can be removed by a finger pad, a rubber ring on the guard or better still by sponge rubber covered with fine black leather.

The left hand should be well forward—just to the tip of the fore-end is preferable—so that, when the gun is mounted to the shoulder, the left arm is well stretched

The first position.

No. II]

The second position.

No. 12]   Front view of the second position.   [30

out (*see* page 29). Be careful to stand firmly on the feet. Stand with the heels touching and the toes about 6–10 inches apart; then move the left foot half-a-step forward and bend the body forward from the hips, so that the chin is over the left toe. This first position (*see* page 28) is a convenient one for mounting the gun quickly to the shoulder (*see* page 29), this stance giving resistance for the recoil of the gun when shooting, allowing the balance to be kept, and enabling the second barrel to be fired quickly and conveniently. Practise mounting the gun to the shoulder in this way.

Authorities differ as to the correct time for pushing forward the safety-slide. Some say, on the score of safety, that this should only be done when a shot is expected, just before or even as the gun is being mounted. Others argue that, whether walking or standing, the gun should always be pointed in a safe direction, and consider that chances will be missed if the slide is not put forward on loading or reloading. Whichever method is followed, the thumb must immediately be moved clear of the slide and opening lever, otherwise a painful injury may follow.

Press the gun to the shoulder with considerable firmness as it is mounted; this should be done in one movement. At the same time press the cheek firmly

Preparing for the first shot at a mark.

against the stock—if the gun is loosely put up, you are likely to suffer from recoil—well back to avoid the nails touching the nose on firing, and always in the same place, although this will vary according to the build of each man.

The eye should be brought into a position about two inches above the stock, keeping both eyes open and facing some object in the room (such as a picture nail)—do this quickly some few times, taking care to come up into the same position every time, with the heel of the butt in line with the top of the shoulder. If you never mount twice alike you cannot expect to shoot well. Avoid dropping the shoulder or tilting the gun, *i.e.*, having one barrel higher than the other.

Have the trigger finger along the guard, for safety, not on the trigger, but ready to fire as soon as the gun is at the shoulder (*see* page 30).

To be able to press the trigger cleanly, the finger should be bent, with the first joint resting lightly on the trigger, so as to prevent a snatch pull; and see that the rest of the finger is not touching the stock, or it will cause the pull to be too heavy, and draw the gun out of alignment.

After working this covering of the object, swing the gun to another selected mark at about 12 to 15 feet to the left of the first ; continue to do this, reversing the movement left to right. Repeat this mode of practice on and off for some days, and then you will be in a position to fire a few shots at a mark in the open, either on a wall, a shot-proof screen made for the purpose (*see* page 32), or a double sheet of your favourite newspaper.

In shooting at such a mark, walk three or four steps towards it before firing ; and never fire if you feel you are not covering the object you desire to hit. This will enable you to observe what you are doing each time, and allow of corrections being made.

When the fixed mark can be hit pretty frequently, the beginner can proceed to practising at moving objects.

JUDGMENT, TIMING AND PULLS.

First among the requisites for successful shooting is judgment of pace or, in other words, of the rate at which the object to be shot is travelling ; then getting the proper allowance, so as to ensure the charge from the gun being put exactly where this moving object is likely to be when the shot reaches it—in the same way as a school-boy learns instinctively by practice, when playing such a game as rounders, where to throw the ball so as to hit or " Scotch " the individual running.

The position of the gun at the moment of taking various types of shot and the actual line of flight of the shot charge are perhaps more clearly shown in the accompanying sketches than they could be in modern photographs. In other words, you are shown " What to do." " How to do it " is, of course, a problem which presents itself for immediate solution with each shot that has to be fired. Unless you are that natural masterpiece, " the born shot," only practice will give you that experience which will instinctively solve the problem in a satisfactory proportion of cases. The rates of flight of game birds and the allowances you must make are discussed later, but it will soon be found that shots taken with a stationary gun aimed the correct distance ahead will result in misses behind. For this reason the article, " Aiming and Allowance," on page 170 should be studied most carefully in conjunction with these earlier chapters. But, in brief, the principle underlying the taking of a successful shot at any angle and in any direction whatever is that the gun must be swung to follow the line of flight and then on through the bird until the correct allowance has been made, particular care being taken not to check the swing at the instant of firing, and to " keep the eye on the bird " even after it has been blotted out by the muzzles in following through.

The sense of touch plays a most important part in shooting. The finger must be pressing the trigger, so that, as the sight and aim complete their share of the work, the shot charge is at the same instant leaving the muzzle. If the pull-off is too hard, time is lost and the judgment beaten; if too light, the gun may be discharged too soon, and possibly not "within a mile" of the place upon which the sight and aim had intended it should be directed to secure the desired impact of the charge of shot on the object to be struck.

The gunmaker has devoted much time to the highly skilled work of making the pulls of the correct weights, which should be about $3\frac{1}{2}$ lbs. for the right lock and 4 lbs. for the left.

Nevertheless, in spite of the word " pull," you must always press the trigger smoothly and never pull or " snatch " it, otherwise you will literally pull the gun out of the correct position for making your shot effective.

CLAY PIGEONS.

Clay (*i.e.*, composition) " pigeons " afford the best means of shooting practice for beginners and in the close season, the latest models of " trap " or thrower being remarkably efficient (*see* page 37).

The trap can be placed so that the clay pigeon will be thrown forward, to the right or left, high or low, or it can be worked by an attendant from behind a wall or shot-proof fence, to imitate closely the flight of driven birds.

The Shooting School is, of course, the ideal place for practice. With scores of traps concealed in natural surroundings, a shot of any conceivable type can be repeated until it is mastered. Nevertheless the interesting and valuable practice to be obtained should on no account be despised or neglected even if conditions permit of the installation of only a " single-rise " trap of one's own.

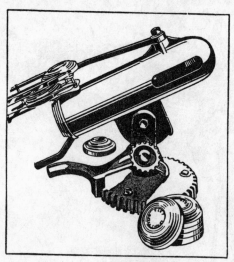

No. 14]   The "Plus" Clay Pigeon Trap

One will not become what is generally known as a " trap-shot " from practising in this way ; but by knowing whence a " bird " will be sprung, a beginner is enabled to become cool and collected, and to take time to see the " flying bird " well on the " wing " before he need shoot—especially if he will walk six to ten paces before having the " bird " released, watch its flight until it has got a fair distance,

Keeping the gun to the shoulder for a " right and left."

and then shoot. Then, when a fair score can be made, two " birds " may be released from separate traps, one just after the other, so as to enable the beginner to get a " right-and-left," and to keep the firing of the second barrel within a fair time of the first. Afterwards both " birds " may be released simultaneously.

Many persons fail in shooting from inability to judge distance. I therefore recommend that, before two " birds " are released, good-sized bunches of newspaper should be left on the ground, say at 30 and 40 yards from where the shooter is standing. With practice this will teach what law a bird should have, and when not to shoot, owing to the bird having flown out of range.

While waiting for a drive to commence it is a good plan to look round and decide the distances away and heights of various trees and bushes so that when game comes you will know at once whether it is within shot. One way is to estimate the longest and shortest distances to the object and to take the average. Another good method is to double the distance of a point judged to be half way. An average two-storey house will be about 30 feet to the ridge of the roof and the so-called " high pheasant " is rarely more than 25 yards up.

Generations of gunmaking efforts have gone to providing two efficient barrels in a gun and you must endeavour to make both tell. Besides the waste of cartridges, you will not be a good shot if you habitually have to apply the experience of a first barrel miss to obtaining a kill with the second barrel. Your position is often easier for the first shot and you must concentrate on killing with it so that you can transfer your attention to a second bird. But do not consider the second until you see you have killed the first.

Do not take the gun down from the shoulder between the two shots (*see* page 38), because it loses much time, and the bird may have flown out of range ; or, in driving, a second shot may be lost in front, the correct and most deadly way to take driven birds.

(It is necessary here to emphasise an exception referred to on page 97. For a " right-and-left " forward *never* take down the gun, but for double shots, one barrel forward and one behind, *always* bring the gun down between the shots. To turn, with the gun at the shoulder, whether following a bird going over or endeavouring to get on to one already passed, endangers other shooters in the line and is most strongly to be discountenanced. After the forward shot, take the gun from the shoulder, turn, planting the feet firmly in the new position, put up the gun and fire, the movements being executed in quick time without haste or flurry.)

MISSING.

A chief cause of missing birds on the wing is the fault of shooting below the object aimed at—the gun not being kept up enough. You must aim above straightforward shots (unless a gun is very straight or too long in the stock), and well ahead or in advance of crossing ones (*see* page 78). There is little fear of shooting too high, or too far in front, if the gun is well brought up to the shoulder; the aim is always too low and too point-blank at first. A sportsman frequently kills much better with his second barrel than with his first, because he instinctively swings his gun further ahead, or raises it over the object to be shot; and also because the hand or trigger-finger obeys the eye quicker, without that perceptible pause which is so fatal to all good shooting. In drawing or pulling the trigger, care should be taken to do it entirely with the finger, and not with any motion of the hand beyond what is involved in squeezing the forefinger and thumb together; or the tendency will be to pull off, in some cases to the right, but often to the left, owing to the gun being pulled across by the extra leverage of the left arm and hand.

When you miss, try and think why you miss; and if you steadfastly keep both eyes open, it will assist you in finding out the cause. If you cannot ascertain the reason, owing to flinching, or closing the eyes at the report of the gun, get someone to load for you, putting an occasional fired case or dummy cartridge in without your knowing when this will be. Then, with the absence of recoil and noise, you will be able to see whether the gun was exactly where you wished it at the moment of pulling the trigger, and, if not, to ascertain and correct the fault. Try this several times in the field, and it will help you considerably. You may be flinching, the instinctive reaction to excessive recoil from an unsuitable gun or cartridges.

This test may be made quietly at crows, magpies, and woodpigeons, without much trouble, or any need to disturb game, as plenty of these birds may be found; but be careful not to mount the gun at them too soon. Be deliberate, particularly if they are well within range; this will greatly assist in lessening that tendency to snap shooting which is so difficult for young sportsmen to overcome. I mean that uncomfortable surprised feeling which puts one off when partridges rise with a whirr, but which never troubles or interferes with a good steady old sportsman, who gives his game plenty of grace, and at the same time is pretty certain of getting a right-and-left out of most rises.

It may happen that after what you felt was a particularly well carried out shot the bird flew on apparently untouched. If there is a succession of such inexplicable misses a few " tracer " cartridges* will be most valuable. These will show you, or better still an observer by your side, exactly where you are going wrong. Provided you are shooting high enough to let the tracer pellet burn out before reaching the ground there is little risk of starting a fire and it is now quite safe to eat game killed with these cartridges.

After an apparent miss-fire be sure to look through the barrels, even if it means losing an easy chance. A defective cartridge may have left a wad in the bore, which would cause a burst when the next shot was fired. A twenty bore cartridge inserted in front of a twelve would cause the same result, so never mix cartridges of different calibres.

---

* At the time of printing these are still not available.

Walking in line to a "point" (Position 1).
Gun well forward—correctly, and safe to others.

ETIQUETTE OF SHOOTING.

A great difficulty here presents itself to the author, because this Treatise is not written with a view to telling the sportsman how shootings should be managed, game reared and found, or ground worked to obtain the best results. Many good works have been written on these subjects, and to them my readers are referred. I will, however, just mention a few of the most important facts to be remembered when shooting in the company of others.

Be careful to carry your gun in such a way that it never covers your left-hand " gun " (*see* pages 44 and 46). It is not pleasant to find the line being broken in walking, owing to the left " guns " hanging back to escape looking down the muzzles of your barrels.

Etiquette of the field often prevents a word of caution being given to a careless man, although a retiring or shrinking away from the line of his gun may have the desired effect (*see* page 47).

In covert, just as much care should be taken, as the careless handling of a gun by one may spoil the enjoyment of a whole party (*see* page 48).

For the same reason do not disturb game by laughing or talking loudly when walking in line, going to your stand or waiting for the drive to commence. You will have earned your invitation if you can persuade the wags and chatterers in the party to be silent at the right times.

No. 17] Walking in line (Position II)—Correctly, and safe to others; barrels well up. [46

No. 18]

Walking in line—Dangerous to others.

No 19]   Standing in covert—Dangerous to others.

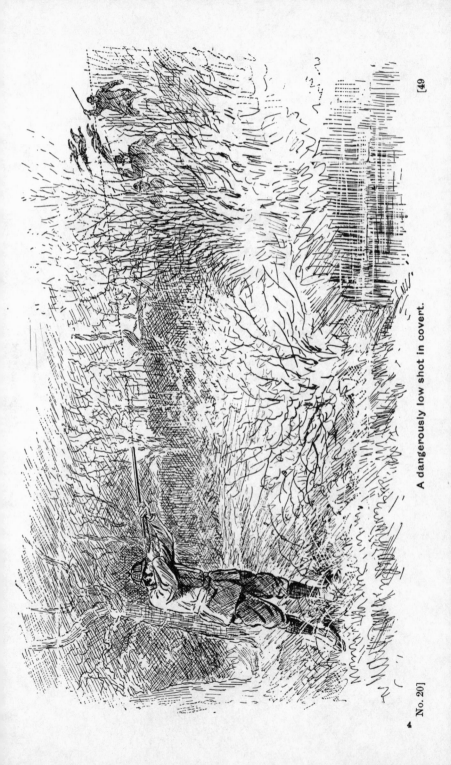

A dangerously low shot in covert.

A dangerous shot.

Always allow pheasants to rise sufficiently to prevent a dangerously low shot being taken (*see* page 49). Although the effective range of a shot-gun is about 40 yards, remember that individual pellets may fly 200 yards or more with sufficient force to wound.

Once one of a party managed to give me a good "dusting" in the following circumstances :—A rabbit was seen in the covert we were facing, when suddenly it bolted out into the ride and came towards me in a direct line. I saw the next "gun" about to shoot. I shouted, "Don't shoot!" but too late; he had fired; the shot glanced from the stony ride and "dusted" me all down one side (*see* page 50).

This shot was made by a man who should have known better; and it so impressed itself on my mind that I cannot help mentioning it here, as a caution to others who might be tempted to fire such a shot.*

---

* Many reports of shooting accidents are published, and a perusal of these emphasises the need for caution not only in the case of beginners but also of those, who " should know better." In the United States the annual casualty lists, as the shooting seasons recur, indicate so large a number of deaths that a correspondent of the *Field* in recording them said : " These figures, representing the results of evident carelessness, suggest that the time must come when something more than the mere desire to 'hunt' will have to be required of those who wish to take out 'hunting licenses'." In this country fatal accidents, though happily not so numerous, do still occur, and it is only by the continual observance of care that they can be avoided.

Many persons may probably have had a similar unpleasant experience.

Never fire at a bird too near ; because, if a kill is made, the game is so dreadfully mangled as not to be worth picking up. And never shoot at too long a range, as the tendency is to wound ; and a bird so struck is seldom recovered, but gets away to die a lingering death. Such shooting is most unsportsmanlike and cruel.

Be careful never to shoot across your next gun nor take his bird (*see* page 52). If, however, you notice that you have " divided " with the next gun an equidistant bird, it may be possible to avoid discomfort or controversy by tactfully delaying or hiding your reloading. If you fire slightly before your neighbour, remember you will hear both shots, but only one may be audible to him.

Cultivate the habit of looking cheerful, particularly at the end of each drive. This costs nothing, helps to induce the frame of mind in which you shoot well, conceals your disappointment if you have done badly, and shows your host, his keepers and beaters your appreciation of their hard work to provide you with sport.

Not where he is, but where he is bolting to.

SHOOTING RABBITS.

This is always good fun, and splendid practice for the beginner, because it teaches him to keep a good look-out, and handle or mount a gun quickly.

Rabbits, as a rule, only give time for a short sight of them. When bolting across a ride, always bear in mind to shoot where they are running to, and not where they are when you first see them (*see* page 54).

Rabbit shooting in rough grass land, or in bracken or furze, is capital sport, if with the assistance of beaters. A perfect line with the guns must be kept, so as to allow of shooting either forward or at rabbits that may break back and run through the line.

A good hedgerow will sometimes hold a great number of rabbits ; and a spaniel or terrier working them, with a gun on either side of the hedge, is good sport at certain seasons—December and January for choice. Great care must be exercised in this sport, so as to avoid wounding the dog or your friend. Remember, as a golden rule, never to shoot at a rabbit on the top of a hedge bank, and on no account be

A quick right and left.

led into shooting into or through a hedge, but let the rabbit be clear and going forward, or back along the outer edge of the ditch, well out in the field. Keep whistling to the " gun " with you, so that you may be opposite each other; and never shoot at a pheasant or any other bird that may be put up if it is crossing to your friend's side of the hedge, but let him shoot when it has got over and clear; simply call to him that something is crossing to his side, so that he may be ready for it.

Rabbits are generally found lying out in tufts of grass in fine weather, and, when started, are certain to make for the hedge or covert (*see* page 56). To make sure of killing them, get well ahead, and shoot at the first chance, because a second is seldom given.

Rabbits are often killed with small bore rifles ; but, although this may be good amusement and at times a necessity, it is not nearly such profitable practice for the beginner as shooting them with a gun. In any case, rifle shooting is outside the scope of this book.

SHORT HERE

Hold well forward.

No 25]

[58

SHOOTING HARES.

Hares in some parts of the country are gradually becoming extinct; and, in the face of the possibility of offending some of my readers, I must frankly say that I think hares should never be shot where it is so, but should be left for those who prefer the sports of beagling and coursing. However, no doubt some of my readers would like to know what to do in the event of their wishing to shoot them.

Hares travel at a great pace and, although a large mark, they are very often missed—or perhaps wounded, getting away to die in a ditch or covert.

To kill cleanly and well a hare running away, the gun should be held well over it (*see* page 58), so as to prevent hitting it in the hind quarters only.

If coming towards the " gun " the aim should be well in front (*see* page 60), and if running across to left or right, especially if it has a clear run up a drain or furrow, plenty of allowance must be given.

A hare should never be shot at a greater distance than 35 to 40 yards, especially if going straight away.

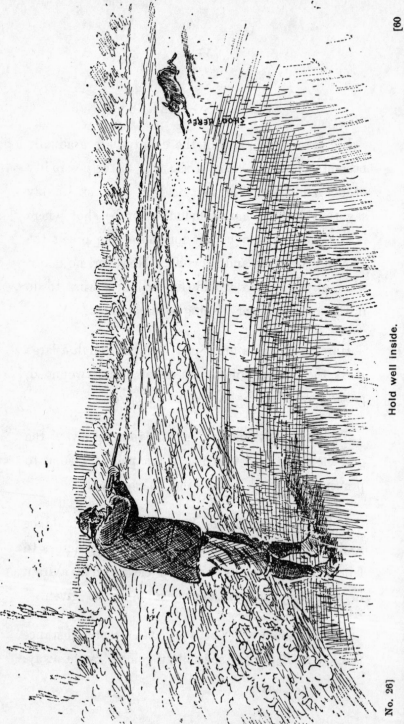

SHOOT HERE!

Hold well inside.

No. 26]

THE "POT" OR SITTING SHOT.

How annoying it is to shoot at an object, such as a crouching wounded bird or a sitting rabbit, that will not move—thus necessitating a "pot" shot—and to find that, even after a considerable amount of preparation, the object fired at has not been touched at all, perhaps even after a second barrel has been discharged.

I have frequently heard the remark, "Oh! you shoot it, So-and-so; I can't hit anything sitting. Make it run or move, and I'm your man." Why is this? Surely it cannot be difficult to shoot at an object perfectly still.

The reason is, I think, this: Very few sportsmen have so studied the question as to know that all shot travels in a paraboloid curve, and under the influence of gravity tends continually to fall below the line of exit from the gun. They are ignorant of the exact "point-blank" range of their gun; and they are not aware that increased or decreased velocity, and variations in the sizes of shot used, will alter the shape of the trajectory curve, although the alterations will be negligible compared with the effect of gravity. Yet these are factors to be taken into consideration,

SHOOT HERE

A sitting or "pot" shot,

No. 27]

and their effect is best determined by actual experiment.

Therefore, at or inside the " point-blank " range of the gun and, with one known load, by shooting just at the point where the object can be seen, or is known, to be touching the ground (*see* page 62), a kill should be a certainty ; whereas at a longer distance the gun must be held above the point of the first aim—sometimes quite over the object to be struck— the shape of the ground being noticed, as to whether the line of fire is level, or up or down hill.

It is useful to make this experiment on a road or path where the shot-marks are clearly visible, by shooting at a turnip, root, or even an old tennis ball.

We can thus understand why, with modern high-velocity rifles, with flat trajectory, more kills are scored than with the old-fashioned ones where the trajectory was very curved—thereby causing the bullet to go over or under, according to the " point-blank " range and the error in sighting or judging of distance by the shooter.

SHOOT HERE

Straight-away shot.

No. 281

THE STRAIGHTFORWARD SHOT.

This class of shot may be considered under three headings—straight-away, high straight-away, and low straight-away shots.

As a rule, the sportsman has time to look well at his bird before putting the gun to his shoulder—especially in the early part of the season, when the cover is good and the birds lie well.

For the straight-away shot, where the bird flies in a bee-line, the gun should be put to the shoulder so that the muzzles blot out the bird. In this case, where the line of flight of the shot coincides with the line of flight of the bird, there is no need for swing, allowance and follow-through (*see* page 64).

If a bird should fly straight, but has risen higher than the shooter, the shot will be taken when the gun appears slightly under—actually ahead of—the bird (*see* page 66).

If a bird on rising flies very low—just skimming away—then the shot is taken when the gun is well over or in advance of the bird (*see* page 67) ; in this class of shot the bird is well blotted out by the muzzles and the tendency is to check the swing and wait a

5

SHOOT HERE

No. 291

High straight-away shot,

Low straight-away and skimming.

No. 30]

[67

SHOOT HERE

The ascending shot—Shoot well over.

No. 31]

fraction of a second too long before firing. Then there is a miss—owing to the shot going where the bird was, instead of where it would have been but for the check and delay.

THE ASCENDING SHOT.

This is a difficult shot, because the general tendency is to shoot too much point-blank at the bird ; whereas, when a bird ascends, it does so at a great pace, and the gun must therefore be mounted and swung very quickly, and be well over the bird (*see* page 68). Here, in fact, almost a " snap " shot is needed.

A pheasant found amongst roots or in a hedge-row often flies almost straight up in a manner very different from that of other game. It is often clean missed or shot in the tail feathers instead of in the head (*see* page 70). Bear in mind, therefore, to shoot well over such a bird, and pull directly the gun is at the shoulder. A moment's delay is sure to cause a failure, to the chagrin of the shooter, who perhaps sees his bird going off with a leg down— if even that ; more likely with only a few feathers gently settling to the ground.

Only tailed.

THE DESCENDING SHOT.

More care is really required in making a clean kill at a descending bird than perhaps at any other; because, as a rule, these shots have to be made on the side of a mountain or hill, where the shooter has only space behind the bird—nothing, in fact, to assist him in judging either distance or pace. And it requires good judgment to realize in a moment that the gun must be so brought to the shoulder as to be slightly under the bird, if going straight away down hill (*see* page 72); or, if to the right or left, slightly in advance—which tends to make the shot more difficult. At the same time, if good clean kills are obtained, nothing looks prettier, or better establishes the reputation of the shooter as being a really first-class shot.

There are times when grouse in crossing a valley fly as shown in the next sketch (*see* page 73); they then present a shot somewhat similar to the low straight-away one (*see* page 67); but as there is nothing to assist the shooter to judge distance they are more difficult, and unless great quickness is shown are soon out of range.

SHOOT HERE.

The down-hill or descending shot.

No. 33]

[72

SHOOT HERE X

No. 34]

Low flying, and crossing a valley.

Position for a snap at a cock.

THE SNAP SHOT.

Snap shots have frequently to be taken at snipe, woodcock and ground game; and to be able to kill well, it is very essential that the gun should fit well, and mount at once to the shoulder with correct alignment. A snap shot can more easily be taken by leaning well forward, so that there is nothing to prevent the gun being brought well up to its place instantaneously (*see* page 74). A man who looks along his gun can never be as good a snap shot as the one who shoots entirely with his eyes fixed on the object he desires to kill. A snap shot may often result in a miss; but what can make up for the delight of a kill when snapping at a woodcock? Nothing, in my humble estimation.

Snap shots at rabbits in cover have frequently to be taken where the rabbit fired at would be concealed by the undergrowth by the time the shot arrived, though well in view at the pulling of the trigger. Such shots are taken into the undergrowth, any hesitation resulting either in a clean miss, or in the useless wounding of the rabbit in the hind-quarters (*see* page 54).

Crossing—a clean right and swinging left.

No. 36]

THE CROSSING SHOT.

This is generally an easy shot; but the beginner must be careful to shoot only at his own birds, *i.e.*, those that really rise to him or cross in front of him, and never to shoot a bird that has crossed to the next gun—whether to the right or left. An outside gun can of course shoot well round (*see* page 76).

It is important to hold well forward and up on birds crossing at or above eye level (*see* pages 78 and 79).

To kill a bird cleanly and well if crossing to the right —generally the more difficult side—get well round, and, if necessary, move the left foot so as to bring the body far enough round, making the right foot the pivot. This will enable the balance of the body to be kept, and admit of the gun being swung ahead again for a second barrel, should the bird be missed with the first (*see* page 80).

No. 37]

SHOOT WELL
AHEAD

Crossing—"Hold well forward."

Well forward and well up—a certain kill.

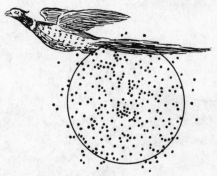

No. 38]   Below and behind—a wounded bird.

These sketches (not to scale) show what correctly and incorrectly taken crossing shots would look like if it were possible for the eye to observe the distribution of shot in flight. They illustrate better than words the importance of keeping well forward and well up to ensure a clean kill. Below and behind is the main reason for birds going away wounded.

Crossing to the right.

Crossing to the left.

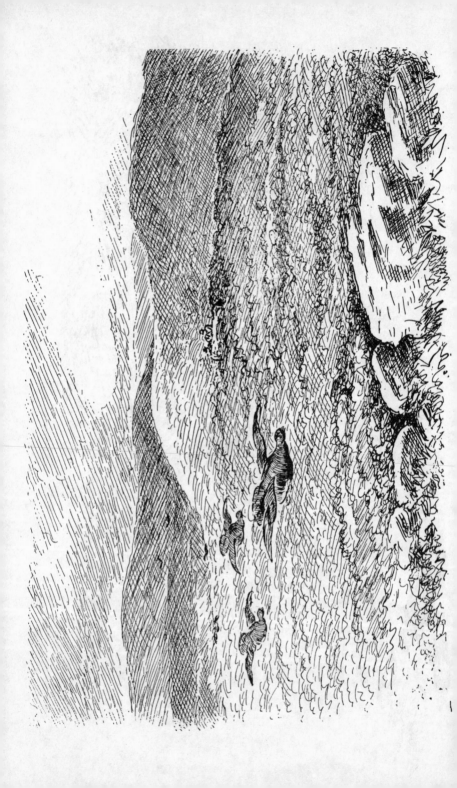

It is not always necessary to move the feet to turn to the left, as it is much easier to swing further and faster to the left than to the right (*see* page 81). An old-time writer of verses on shooting, who reasoned better than he rhymed, expressed it thus :—

> " The birds that left-ward fly are miss'd the least,
> As you'll soon find, that 'tis the easiest
> Direction that the gun can be controlled ;
> But either way, it can't too oft be told
> The Novice, that unless the piece he moves
> As with the bird it were, but fruitless proves
> Th' attempt——"

In driving, crossing shots become more difficult, especially at driven grouse when flying low (*see* page 82), as the tendency is to shoot very much over as well as behind—therefore bear in mind to get forward and well down to your bird, because of the fact that one is apt to give excessive elevation by keeping the eye too much above the breech of the gun.

The velocity of flight of a bird must be quickly judged—more in crossing shots than in any other ; and an allowance of from three to even eight feet or more must be made, according to the pace of the bird and the distance it is away from the gun.* At the longer

* See AIMING AND " ALLOWANCE," page 170.

distances the aim must also be a little higher, so as to allow for the drop of the shot, which travels in a curve owing to the pull of gravity.

Particularly with crossing shots, however, it must be realized that because a bird is near it is not necessarily easy. The angular velocity of a bird at 20 yards will be twice as great as that of one flying at the same pace at 40 yards. In other words, it will be crossing your front at twice the rate. Not only will you have less time to mount your gun, but you will have to swing it twice as fast to get on to the bird. It will of course be understood that this *rate* of swing is quite distinct from the *amount* of allowance, although naturally the brain and muscles have to take both factors into consideration at the same time.

THE QUARTERING SHOT.

It will be realized that, when a bird gets up, it is, more often than not, flying at an oblique angle ; and a quartering shot is usually more difficult than a crossing one.

Care must be taken, with shots of this class, to give less allowance in front than in actual crossing shots. The reason is not far to seek. The diagonal flight of a bird quartering to left or right represents a combination of the straight-away and crossing flight. The crossing bird requires a full allowance in front, while the straight-away bird does not need, and cannot have, any. The quartering shot, therefore, calls for an allowance between the two, less or more as the angle is more or less straight-away. In addition, allowance must be made for rising, if the flight is upwards.

A partridge which looks to be flying straight very often inclines its flight to right or left and needs at least a little leading if it is not to fly clear of the shot. Upon this point the late Sir R. Payne-Gallwey gives this useful hint : " It is well for a shooter to know that, though a bird may, to all appearance, be flying directly from him, if its head can be seen it is really flying towards the side on which the head appears."

To approaching quarterers similar reasoning applies.

SHOOT HERE

No. 42]

[86

The approaching high shot.

THE APPROACHING SHOT.

This shot forms the basis of driving, and may be divided into three kinds—the approaching high shot, *i.e.*, above the level of the sportsman's head, the approaching low shot, *i.e.*, below the level of his head, and the direct, *i.e.*, straight on.

The high approaching shot must be made by shooting well in front of the bird's head (*see* page 86). A bird approaching at a lower altitude does not need quite so much allowance, although it may be further away, because the line of flight of the bird and the path of the shot more nearly coincide.

As in crossing shots, near birds are likely to be harder. It is effective to see a fairly high pheasant well taken, but for sheer difficulty it is hard to beat the covey of partridges which comes bustling over a ten-foot hedge and on seeing you explodes in all directions. Then you have to swing with a vengeance and only the cool, quick, well-schooled man will kill.

The approaching low shot in partridge driving, where the hedge behind which the shooter is standing is lower than his shoulders, is also difficult, because

A nice angle to take at.

the bird is often fired at when too far from the gun, or sometimes when much too near.

In shooting at an approaching low-flying bird, the shooter must get his gun well down and under the bird, or he will miss it by firing over—really behind it. Many birds are missed in this way owing to the fact that the gun is not brought high enough up on the shoulder (*see* page 90).

To kill well a bird which is flying directly at the shooter's head, cover it with the muzzles (*see* page 91), and then pull at once, so as not to let it get too close.

Anyone accustomed to shooting young driven grouse from behind a wall will grasp my meaning. They come skimming along, very low and straight at the gun, and the size or perspective is the only evidence of speed and distance. If you fire when your bird is looking as big as a blackbird, you may kill with nearly every shot, but miss that moment, and you will not kill any. To be more exact, you should try to fire when the bird is 40 yards out. In another second he will be almost 20 yards nearer you, and a second is not a long period of time.

SHOOT HERE

The approaching low shot.

No. 44]

SHOOT HERE

The approaching direct shot.

No. 45]

[91]

Shooting well back overhead

THE PERPENDICULAR SHOT.

A bird taken well overhead, or perfectly perpendicular, is one of the most telling and prettiest shots to be made (*see* page 92), but one requiring great coolness and practice. When learnt, however, such a shot is not difficult, as by waiting it gives plenty of time to get ready—the bird having been seen, at some distance away, as it approaches.

When shot in this way birds are more often well killed, as they present the most vulnerable parts to the shooter. If birds are flying at a great pace and high, a good allowance in front must be made or they will be missed. Yet although the height necessitates a large allowance, it also calls for a corresponding reduction in the rate of swinging the gun.*

Standing perfectly steady (*see* page 94), and watching the bird approach until it is nearly overhead, the body must then be thrown back so that the whole of the weight is on the right leg, the left toes just touching the ground, so as to steady the shooter (*see* page 95), the left hand being brought down the barrels nearer to the right, so as to allow the gun to be kept in the correct position, right shoulder—right eye—line of sight ; otherwise it will be drawn to the left, and so be out of proper alignment, causing the shot to go to the left.

* If the reason for this has not already been made clear, reference should again be made to page 170.

Watching them coming high—back from roots into covert.

How to get them well overhead.

Few sportsmen are seen to take this class of shot really well. Many fail because they do not practise the movement sufficiently before they go out, and consequently do not get far enough back —being too stiff; also, because, even if they do get far enough ahead of the bird at the instant of pulling, they check the gun perceptibly.

Useful practice may be had by placing a clay bird trap on a hay-rick or out-building and then sending the clay pigeons well over the shooter's head, the shooter facing the trap; but far better facilities are, of course, available at Shooting Grounds, at some of which there are specially constructed towers up to 120 feet high from which clay birds can be projected at great speed and in any direction.

These Grounds are excellently equipped for game shooting practice of all kinds. In Part II the subject is more fully dealt with, so that further reference to it here is unnecessary.

THE APPROACHED AND PASSED SHOT.

This kind of shot often presents itself, especially in partridge driving when the beaters are getting well up to the guns. The birds cannot then be shot as they approach, for fear beaters should be peppered.

If a bird flying high has to be shot after it has passed overhead, the shooter must turn round and get well under the bird, that is, ahead of it, to prevent shooting behind. This is an easy shot where one can look well over the gun, because the muzzle is swung right under the bird, which is never lost to view (*see* page 99).

If a passed bird has flown low between the guns, the shooter must get well over or ahead of it. This is more difficult than the higher shot, as the bird is more or less hidden by the gun, as it is flying under the line of sight until the moment of firing (*see* pages 100 and 101). In turning to shoot at a bird after it has passed, never allow the gun to cover your neighbour, but take it down from the shoulder until *after* you have faced completely round, and then re-mount it (*see* pages 98–101, and note on page 40).

7

This illustration is intended to show—Right, How an approaching high bird is to be taken; Left, How the same bird would be

C.HEPYCHEP.SC.

SHOOT HERE

No. 50]

Approached and passed high shot.

[100]

Approached and passed low shot (1)—A quick right.

No. 51

Approached and passed (II)—and useful left.

No. 52]

[101

No. 53]   [No. 54.

Shooting with a pair of guns.

SHOOTING WITH A PAIR OF GUNS.

This Treatise has been prepared rather as a primer than as a work embracing each and every phase of instruction necessary, but I have been requested by many of my patrons to include a few lines about "Shooting with a Pair of Guns and a Loader." Accordingly the illustrations, Nos. 53 and 54, page 102, have been prepared to give an idea of what is required.

For choice, the loader should stand just behind the right-hand shoulder facing the same direction as the " gun ". He should be well prepared with a stock of cartridges conveniently carried in a bag, an assistant having a further supply for replenishing the bag between drives.

The gun he is holding should be in his right hand with muzzles up and slightly sloped to the left. After his " gun " has fired either one or both barrels, the loader should take the discharged gun with the left hand, passing the second gun, which he has loaded in readiness, with the right hand holding the small of the stock only, and taking the fired gun with the left hand by the barrels, and the " gun " should take the loaded gun from the loader also with his left hand. The drill is practically that each shall " take with the left hand."

The " gun " should at all times, before handing his gun to the loader, pull the safety slide back, so that the word " SAFE " is exposed, the loader having nothing to do with it. Should the " gun " forget to do this, I would suggest that the loader be instructed to warn him that he has not done so ; otherwise should only one barrel be fired, he would be passing back to the loader a gun loaded in one barrel, and ready to fire, a *very* dangerous proceeding.

The loader, on receiving the gun, should face sufficiently to the rear, turning the barrels well away from the shooting line to prevent anyone being covered in the act of opening the gun for the fired cases to be ejected, or while re-loading, and should not face about until the gun is properly closed, then see that the barrels are pointing upwards, and held in the original position.

Neither while holding the gun nor in handing it back must the loader push forward the safety slide. This point is stressed because, being so obvious, it might easily be overlooked in training a new loader.

After each " stand " or " drive " the loader must remove all cartridges from the barrels, and not re-load until his " gun " has arrived at the next " stand " or position.

I would suggest that a loader should have with him a cartridge extractor, of the spring clip or universal pattern. A knife and some string are usefully included in the odds and ends a shooter carries.

———

PART II.

———

The previous pages of this work treat of the practical part of the Art of Shooting, dealing with the means which the sportsman should adopt, under the varying conditions of the bird's flight, to use his gun with effect. Now it is proposed to devote some further space to remarks on the gun and its accessories, and matters of a more or less theoretical character. First among the subjects to be considered will be

CLOTHES.

In looking round at those about to join in a day's shooting, it does not take long for the practised eye to detect which are the sportsmen and which are the tailor's models. It is simply astonishing at times to imagine why some of the materials, with their rainbow colours and mixtures, should ever have been designed and made.

Clothing should be chosen to resemble the natural surroundings of the shoot, and for ordinary purposes of sport, dull neutral shades best serve to make the shooter inconspicuous.

In the early part of the season, when fair and warm weather are looked for, the light weatherproofed materials make very comfortable and durable shooting clothes, but later in the year the heavier tweeds or homespuns give the warmth then required and are decidedly preferable. At all times warm underclothing should be worn, for in every kind of shooting there is waiting as well as walking.

Clothes should be cut so as to fit well, but at the same time to permit the sportsman to handle his gun freely in any position, and not to impede his movements. Badly-cut clothes, too tight across the back or in the sleeves, often prevent a man shooting well.

A well-cut jacket and loosely-cut breeches or knickerbockers are the best for sport generally. To some extent fashion has to be consulted even in shooting dress, but too much weight should not be attached to it. Comfort and freedom in action are all-important.

The garments known as " plus fours " should be avoided. They may be suitable for the game from which their name is derived, but a short walk through long grass even on a fine Autumn morning will give you rolls of heavy, clammy cloth round the knees for the rest of the day. But to make sure of their unsuitability get them really wet in soaking rain and then go along the edge of a ploughed field and through a barbed wire fence to your position for the next drive !

Good boots, in which the feet are perfectly comfortable, are most essential. I defy any man to shoot well or enjoy his day if his feet are galled or blistered.

It is wise to have boots large enough to allow of wearing a pair of thick socks as well as your stockings. This will help to keep the feet at the proper temperature, prevent chafing, and the nails which infest boots are less likely to work into your skin. Before starting your shooting see that the studs in the soles and heels are up to their work and if necessary have them renewed but never start a long day on the hills or fields in new boots—it has been done very often with most saddening results. New boots should be broken in gradually well in advance. Stout shoes may be preferred early in the season.

However good your raincoat and boots may be it is likely that at the end of a wet day the rain will have run down your legs and given you wet feet. It is therefore a very good thing to bring dry shoes and stockings and a warm overcoat for the drive home.

A close-fitting comfortable cap is often worn, with peak at front to shade the eyes. Its shape must, almost of necessity, vary from time to time, though changes are made so gradually that it is only in looking at old photographs of shooting groups (or at the sketches in this book) that one realises the " impossibility " of the caps that used to be worn. In precisely the same way the head-gear of the present may be relied on to cause amusement to future generations, but upon one point, which photography does not bring out, there will be agreement. Whatever the shape, and whether you prefer a soft felt hat, a cap or the effective and now revived "deer-stalker," the colour must be inconspicuous, for the covering of the head is first seen by birds in driving, and, if too conspicuous, it will turn the birds from you. A bare, white forehead is even worse.

A shooting seat is a desirable adjunct to the equipment. There are many patterns to choose from, and the only suggestion that need here be made concerning them is that, being designed to serve both as a walking-stick and a seat, the one selected should be more of a seat than a walking-stick. There is nothing more uncomfortable than attempting to sit on the handle of a walking-stick !

A cartridge bag should of course be water-proof and one stiffened to keep the mouth well open is desirable. The everlasting wear of a first-class leather one well repays the initial cost.

SHOT GUN CALIBRES.

The sporting gun of the present day retains many traces of its ancient origin. The term " bore," used to indicate calibre, is a survival from times when facilities for fine measurements were not generally available, and, in the making of firearms, were not greatly needed. The old sizes of bore were based upon the actual diameters of spherical balls of lead. Thus a 12-bore is a barrel bored to take a lead ball weighing $\frac{1}{12}$th of a pound. Balls for 20-bores run twenty to the pound, 4-bores four to the pound, and so on. The fact that spherical ball has become practically obsolete, and that if bullets are intended to be shot from smooth barrels at all they generally do not agree with the old standard of weight, does not affect the question of nomenclature. The old, expressive, well understood and convenient term " bore " is universally adhered to when shot-guns are spoken of. There is an exception made in the case of such small sizes as the .410, but for this a good reason exists. The old list of gauges ended at 50-bore and balls running 50 to the pound required a .453 diameter of tube. There is, therefore, no real " bore " small enough to correspond with .410, and 28-bore is the smallest " bore " for which cartridges are now available.

PHASES OF DEVELOPMENT.

Indications of the influence of the past throw light upon the processes by which the modern gun has been developed. From the beginning the primary purpose has been the same— to enable the shooter to hit the object at which he aims. In comparison with that everything else is subordinate. The outline, proportions and balance of a gun are determined on a basis affected only in detail by individual preferences. They have been arrived at as the result of a consensus of opinion resulting from processes of selection and rejection which have gone on literally for centuries. By the test of long experience, the most suitable survives and becomes a type.

The outlines of the gun, with its just proportions for handling, aiming, and for firing by means of a trigger, had been symmetrically determined long before the breech-loader, with expansive cartridge case, came into existence. From that time onwards, gunmakers, in adopting the various improvements in mechanism which the breech-loader brought in its train, have endeavoured to combine them with the contours and characteristics of the best types of muzzle-loader. This was not done from æsthetic motives, for in reality it was the only course open which could be followed with reasonable prospects of success. Breech-loading is the greatest improvement in gunmaking ever introduced, but the advantage of a breech-loader over a muzzle-loader lies in the loading, not in the firing. With the cap in the cartridge, instead of on the nipple outside the gun, ignition might be quickened a little, and charges prepared beforehand were likely to be more serviceable than those loaded up with the aid of flasks and a ramrod in the field, but these, at best are minor matters, for it would have been hopeless to expect that a gun which *loaded* better could ever entirely supersede a gun which *shot* better. The advantage of quick and easy loading was enormous, and to get rid of the ramrod was worth any sacrifice except a sacrifice of shooting qualities. Loading is a means to an end, but shooting is the end itself.

HAMMER AND HAMMERLESS GUNS.

The hammered breech-loader, as it was slowly perfected, became so like the muzzle-loader that, at the shoulder, one kind could hardly be distinguished from the other. When the hammerless was introduced a definite change was brought about. As that occurred not so many decades ago it is hardly necessary to recall the very well-known fact that a great many shooters did not like it. There were arguments reasonably urged against the hammerless, but perhaps the most powerful, though with the least to say for itself, was the instinctive feeling that without hammers the gun did not look right. We may call that prejudice, but there was reason behind it. If hammers ought not to have been on the outside of a gun they, or their equivalents, would certainly not have remained there for centuries. In gunmaking, there is a reason for everything.

The reason why the cock and hammer of a flint lock, or the cock and nipple of a percussion gun, were placed outside was that, though many attempts were made, no really successful way was ever found of making them work inside. When the actual means of ignition, the cap, became a part of the charge, the old difficulties disappeared, and the change was accordingly made. It was then urged that external hammers served a useful purpose in guiding the eye. It may be that, for those who held the belief, they did. The hammer breech-loader is still occasionally made, but the verdict of contemporary opinion overwhelmingly favours the hammerless system. Finally the ejector, to throw out the empty shells of fired cartridges, gained acceptance on similarly sound lines by quickening reloading without interfering in any way with the primary purpose of the gun or marring its symmetry of form.

The intention to refrain from any detailed description of gun mechanisms, extends, of course, to the productions of this firm. In 1826, the first Lancaster guns were fitted with flint and steel locks. At that time, detonators and percussion cap guns were coming into use and attention was almost immediately directed upon these. Lancaster had had the advantage of working for the celebrated Joseph Manton, and his own productions followed generally the Manton lines. The percussion muzzle-loader had barely reached its full development when, in 1852, the Lefaucheux drop-down breech-loader, with pin-fire cartridges, was introduced in England by Joseph Lang, who had started in business in 1821. In 1853, Lancaster brought out the first central-fire breech-loader, with which a cartridge having fulminate in the base itself, instead of in a cap, was originally used. The central-fire capped cartridge led to the general adoption of the C.F. system with which the firm has been intimately associated.

CYLINDER AND CHOKE BORING.

Before the system was devised of controlling the spread of shot by choke boring, it was universally believed that all shot-guns made their patterns too wide. With the old cylinder-bored guns, which were not true cylinders, being opened or relieved for some part of their length, shooters took, or imagined they took, very long shots indeed. Missing these shots, they said, with perfect truth, that the pattern was too scattered, and clamoured for guns to shoot closer. It seems to have been overlooked that already at easy distances the guns shot quite closely enough, or more probably the fact was not recognised that a good close pattern a long way off must of necessity have for its accompaniment a bad, or, at any rate, a bunched-up, pattern at the nearer distances.

The relative points of chokes or cylinders are here touched upon, not with a view to advocating the one or the other, but of showing the difference between them. A " cylinder " barrel is a straight tube, of nearly the same diameter throughout from end to end, but often relieved at muzzle and breech. The " choke " barrel is a tube the front part of which is narrower or contracted in the last two inches to the muzzle. This narrowing consists of a tapering section, known as the cone, giving a reduction of up to 40 thousandths of an inch in dia-meter, and varying in length according to the degree of choke. Between cone and muzzle is another parallel part of the bore, shorter or longer as there is less or more choke.

The penetration is so nearly equal with one boring or another that it is needless to go further into that aspect of the matter here. A great many trials have been made to settle the point, but for practical purposes it is generally admitted that the difference is immaterial. The patterning properties need a little more attention. A distance of 40 yards is adopted as the standard range for patterning sporting guns, the number of pellets striking within a 30-inch circle being counted, and often expressed as a percentage of the complete charge. It will not, of course, be overlooked that the precise number of pellets on a given space is relatively of less importance than the manner in which those pellets are distributed. A cluster pattern interspersed with open spaces through which a bird could escape might count better, but be much worse, than a well-distributed pattern, which expressed as a percentage would reveal none of the good qualities seen on the plate. It will be remembered also that a thin pattern at 40 yards must have opened up from a thicker 30 yards pattern which at 20 yards was probably on the close side ; while the pattern still held nicely together at 40 yards must at the nearer distances have had so narrow a spread as to reduce greatly the chances of hitting.

In a word, one cannot have it both ways. Barrels may be bored to combine with good patterns at one range still useful patterns as the range increases, but the tendency of the charge is always to spread and the most that can be done is to maintain an adequate killing circle over as great a distance as possible. At short ranges the true cylinder gives the widest killing circles, and the best chances. For long shots, the full choke has an undoubted superiority, with countervailing disadvantages at the nearer distances.

SCALE of CHOKES for SHOTGUNS

Adopted by the Gunmakers' Association

	12-Bore	16-Bore	20-Bore	Percentage Patterns to be Expected
TRUE CYLINDER	·729	·662	·615	40
QUARTER CHOKE	·719	·653	·607	55
HALF CHOKE	·709	·644	·599	60
THREE-QUARTER CHOKE	·699	·635	·591	65
FULL CHOKE	·689	·626	·583	70
There is also the intermediate boring known as Improved Cylinder, with a constriction of ·004″				50

OLD GUNS AND NITRO PROOF.

Although Nitro Proof has only been compulsory since 1925, most gunmakers had as a matter of course submitted their guns voluntarily since about 1905, by which year the use of smokeless powders was quite usual. Even a best gun made since then has had plenty of time to be ruined by neglect, but there are still many thousands about proved only for black powder and many of these are in a deplorable condition. Therefore never buy a gun except from, or with the advice of, a reputable maker or gun dealer, whose knowledge and reputation will ensure that you are not let down. If you have a gun proved only for black powder, get a gunmaker to submit for nitro proof. It may burst, but it is far better that this should be at the Proof House than in the field. The Rules of Proof require that guns submitted shall be tight at the breech and with the barrels free from dents and bulges, and the charges for the necessary work and for proof (at owner's risk) are of course payable whether the gun passes proof or not.

Apart from Black Powder guns, there are many which were Nitro Proved when made of which the chambers have been deepened or of which the barrels have by neglect or damage and repair been enlarged out of the category in which they were proved. They have thus become unproved and reproof is necessary.

No discussion of the Proof Act is necessary in a book of this sort beyond the statement that it is intended purely for the protection of the user of a gun, and any benefits conferred on the gunmaker are incidental. The Worshipful Company of Gunmakers, London, and the Guardians of the Birmingham Proof House are charged with carrying out the proof tests without passing which no new gun may be offered for sale. For his own sake, the shooter should see that his gun is in good condition, and bears on the barrels near the breech one of the following marks, indicating that it has passed Nitro Proof.

NITRO PROOF

For further information on Proof, readers are referred to the new Rules of Proof, 1954, superseding those of 1925, and to "Notes on the Proof of Gun Barrels." These and advice on Proof are obtainable from the Proof Master at the Proof Houses at 48, Commercial Road, London, E.1, and Banbury Street, Birmingham, 5.

The subject is also treated at some length in Major Sir Gerald Burrard's excellent book "The Modern Shotgun."

THE MODERN GUN.

Under this heading it is not intended to dictate to the accomplished shot, whose views are already formed by experience, but to help the beginner by indicating the mould in which centuries of development have cast present gunmaking practice and the departures from it which may be useful in certain cases.

The controversies which have burned so fiercely in the last fifty years have naturally left their mark on the modern gun, but while this is not the place to recapitulate them, reference might perhaps be permitted to the metal out of which barrels are made. "Damascus" or "gun-barrel iron" was in use for many generations and the beautiful figure and colour contrasts of old barrels are still a delight to the eye. That bursts were not frequent is a great tribute to the skill and excellent workmanship of the old barrel filers in producing such a heterogeneous material. But the primitive and tedious methods of production involved could not survive against the advances, particularly since 1914, in our knowledge of steel, which is the same all through. To the sorrow of many, the question "Damascus or Steel" has been settled by the fact that the former is not now made in this country, and is probably not in commercial production, in good quality, anywhere in the world.

Although barrels are universally made of steel now, there remains considerable diversity in length. Since 1920 the vast majority have been 28 inches long, although more than this length is often required and many hold shorter barrels in favour, as quite a number did in 1875. This applies to 12 bores ; in smaller bores 28 inch barrels are often felt to give rather a " billiards-cue " effect and 26 inches is the preferred length. Of course the length of stock required must be considered in fixing the barrel length to give a properly proportioned gun.

Barrels are usually bored right improved cylinder, left half choke, giving patterns of about 140 and 160, respectively, for preference. If two guns are to be used much for driving it may be best to have all four barrels bored the same, and improved cylinders will probably be the most suitable.

The weight of a 12 bore has been reduced from the time when black powder propelled $1\frac{1}{8}$ oz. of shot from a 7 lb. gun. $6\frac{1}{4}$ lbs. to $6\frac{1}{2}$ lbs. can be accepted as the present standard, while down to 6 lbs. is not uncommon. There are now made guns to take only the 12 bore 2 inch paper cartridge firing $\frac{7}{8}$ oz. shot and these weigh about $5\frac{1}{4}$ lbs. The 2 inch metal cartridges with full shot charge are not intended for such guns, and although the guns themselves may stand the strain, the heavy recoil will punish the user.

The power of guns is strictly proportional to the shot charges used and less powerful guns are available, such as 16, 20 and 28 bores, right down to the .410, which is quite effective for a boy starting to shoot.

For high-grade guns, the side-lock action is almost invariably used, whereas in the lower qualities the box-lock allows of the production of a better gun at a given price. The under-lever is now restricted to the heaviest types of shoulder gun and the top lever is the most widely used type, though the side lever action so popular on Stephen Grant guns ever since 1866 still has many faithful adherents.

Of ejectors and lock-work it is hardly necessary to speak as there is scarcely a gun made which is not of sound design, whatever its shortcomings may be in other directions. Hand-detachable and attachable locks have advantages for the man overseas who may be a thousand miles from a so-called "gunsmith", but generally, the internal mechanism of a gun is best left to the ministrations of the expert. One does not interfere with the inside of a watch !

The "under and over" principle is probably as old as the use of two barrels in a gun and many users find considerable advantage in modern applications of the idea. For technical reasons these guns are more expensive to make than the side by side variety and have certainly suffered in popularity from the clumsy appearance and handling of certain makes, notably from abroad.

The single trigger again is an eighteenth century idea, not developed then owing to an incomplete understanding of the principles involved. After the advent of the hammerless ejector, single triggers were quite common but latterly the many unsatisfactory systems have reacted to the detriment of the few good ones and double triggers are again in the great majority.

Apart from its other advantages, in cases of disability the single trigger often offers the only solution to an individual's problem, but it must be remembered that all other conditions being equal, a mechanism with a greater number of parts must have a greater inherent liability to derangement.

Whatever the specification of a gun, the safety mechanisms must be satisfactory. The thumb-piece on top must be bold enough to allow of easy use when the hands are cold yet it should not be so large as to be in the way at other times. When it is in the back position, with the word " SAFE " showing, the triggers are bolted so that they cannot be pulled. See that in any gun you ever use this position is taken up automatically every time the lever is moved to open the gun. A gun with a " non-automatic " safety may be safe in the hands of an experienced shot accustomed to it, but otherwise may be highly dangerous. There is also the device known as the " intercepting sear," designed to prevent the fall of the tumbler upon the striker except as the result of the trigger having been pulled.

In all the foregoing, it has of course only been possible to express generalities and your particular requirements will in the end be determined by your physical characteristics. Your shooting friend may not be qualified to say what your needs are, even if experience has taught him to know his own more or less intuitively. Therefore, if you are buying a gun, consult a gunmaker who applies to his building and fitting a first-hand knowledge of what happens in the field.

GUN CLEANING.

When black powder was in use, it made the bores of guns look very much dirtier than smokeless powder does, but delay in cleaning did less harm. The fouling, or even the apparent absence of fouling, following the use of nitro powders, should be dealt with as soon as possible after firing. While shooting is going on, the passage of tightly-fitting wads along the bore clears out much of the residue left by the preceding shot, fresh fouling being deposited behind, for removal in its turn. The more complete combustion of nitro powders, in comparison with black, explains the cleaner appearance of the bore after shooting, the elimination of smoke and the diminution of fouling being attributable to the same cause. Whether the visible evidences are plentiful or slight, the inside of the barrel, after the passing along it of flaming gas, is left coated with a residual film, more or less corrosive in its nature. Cleaning, which need not be a very lengthy process as there are only plain surfaces to be dealt with, ought to be seen to as soon as possible after returning from shooting in order effectively to remove the fouling and neutralise the tendency of rust to form.

If the gun has been out in the wet or snow, it should be well wiped over with a soft rag the same evening at the latest, and not be allowed to remain till the following morning, when rust will have formed. Blotting paper is useful for getting water out from beside the ribs, and from other places where the rag will not remove it easily.

Assuming the outside to be dry (or dried), the following is the best plan :—

To remove all leading, fouling and general dirt after a day's shooting, proceed thus :—Screw the jag on to the cleaning rod, of which the handle should be small enough to pass easily right through the barrels, and then put on it dry tow or clean patches so that it will enter the barrel fairly tightly. Do not use any oil at all this time, as the absence of oil enables the tow to grip the dirt well, and removes it very quickly if the rod is passed from breech to muzzle briskly a few times. Another good way is to ram suitable sized wads of tow through in the same direction with the handle end of the rod.. After using the rod, look through the barrel to see if clean ; if not, continue the operation a little longer, and if necessary increase the amount on the jag to make it fit the barrel more tightly. If some fouling still remains, it should be removed with a bristle brush. Wire brushes unless liberally oiled may do more harm than good. If it has been necessary to use a brush, the barrels must again be cleaned out as before. Then see that the fronts of the chambers are clean, particularly if you have been using cartridges shorter than the chambers (for instance $2\frac{1}{2}$ inch case cartridges in a $2\frac{3}{4}$ inch gun). The muzzles and the recesses to take the cartridge rims should be wiped clean.

A new wool mop should have a daily dose of Rangoon oil until it is thoroughly impregnated, after which it will only need an occasional application. If you examine the mop you will see that the wool spreads upwards and outwards from the threaded end and will rapidly come away if pushed against the grain through the barrel. Therefore *pull* it twice through each barrel from breech to muzzle, slowly, so as to deposit as much of the oil as will remain. Never use the mop for anything but this oiling—if used for cleaning it will quickly become foul and useless.

In wiping out the barrels, the muzzles should never be placed on a stone or concrete floor.

The gun should always be looked at two or three days after it has been put aside, when if any fouling has been left it will have become visible.

When the barrels are finished inside, carefully wipe clean the face of the action, which will otherwise soon show signs of corrosion round the striker holes, and any other part requiring attention. Rangoon oil or vaseline, well worked on and into a soft piece of rag or an old pocket-handkerchief, is the best thing for cleaning all the outside parts of a gun, such as outsides of barrels (after the insides have been carefully wiped out), lock-plates, breech-action, triggers and guard, and other parts of metal that are exposed. *Never* allow oil to be applied by a feather, or any brush that is likely to deposit the oil too liberally.

The great fault is putting too much oil on a gun, so that it gets gummy, or clogs the working, more especially of hammerless ejectors. Linseed oil is particularly liable to clog the mechanism and must be avoided. A superfluity of oil also attracts any grit which may be about. If a gun will not go together easily and shut properly, always suspect that dirt is preventing two surfaces from coming together as they should.

It is best to send guns to their makers, or to some practical maker, at the end of each season, certainly before the next commences, for overhaul and cleaning.

The shooter would be saved much inconvenience and annoyance if this were done regularly. Guns are worn out not by use but by abuse and neglect. For instance, the passage of shot over dents in barrels will in time wear the metal thin and perhaps even into holes.

A good gun is worth taking care of personally but in addition to the attention you should give it yourself and the annual overhaul, it is well worth while to pay the small premium necessary for insurance against loss or damage, including bursting of barrels and breakage of the stock. For a further small sum you can also provide against any claim arising if you should be so unfortunate as to " pepper " somebody.

SIGHT AND ITS PECULIARITIES.

To become an average shot, it is first absolutely necessary to be able to see clearly any object up to, say, 50 yards.

Those who cannot otherwise see to shoot should use spectacles having the glasses made either to follow the shape of the orbits or circular with a diameter of not less than $1\frac{1}{2}$ inches, and with the lower parts well set out from the face, so that, when the head is in the correct position with the gun at the shoulder, the surfaces of the glasses are at right angles to the line of sight. Then it must be ascertained which eye is the master, or, in other words, whether it is the right or left eye that finds the object the more quickly and sees it the better.

This may be determined by pointing at an object with the arm and finger extended and both eyes open. If on closing the left eye the finger is in line with the object then the right is the master, as will be confirmed by closing the right and opening the left, when the finger will be found to point to the left of the object. Conversely the left eye will control the pointing if it is the master.

No man with a left eye more powerful than the right can be expected to take a correct alignment with the right eye, nor can any man shoot accurately with a gun unless the centre of the rib of the barrels comes absolutely opposite his master eye. If he has a right-eyed gun, the left being the master eye, it will cause him to shoot from 1 to 6 feet to the left of the object according to its distance away. What happens in such a case is clearly shown in the illustration on page 126. The breech

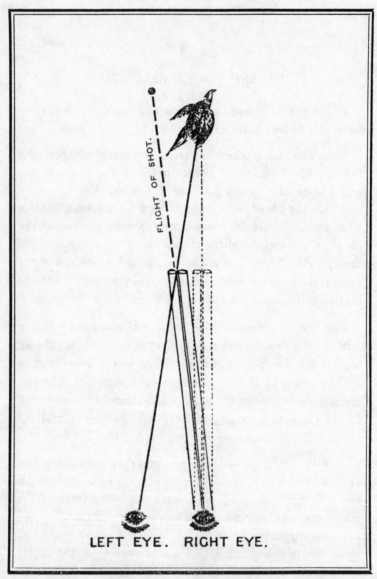

FLIGHT OF SHOT.

LEFT EYE.   RIGHT EYE.

Effect of aiming with both eyes open, the left being
the master eye.

end of the barrels is correctly positioned but the stronger left eye has taken charge and pulled the muzzles over to its line of sight. This only depicts what happens with a stationary object. In shooting at an object crossing from R to L the left-eyed shooter would be ahead of it, and with a better chance of hitting it, but if crossing from L to R he would be a great deal behind, and consequently miss it.

I find, since the publication of the early Editions, that the solution has sorely puzzled many sportsmen, therefore I give the following suggestions, hoping that they may assist those having a more powerful left eye : 1. Shoot from the left shoulder and left eye, the gun being specially constructed for this purpose. 2. Close the left eye before the gun is put to the shoulder, so as to allow of the right eye "fixing" or thoroughly observing the object. Another method (3) is to interpose a screen between the foresight and the left eye. This may take the form of a patch on the left lens if glasses are worn, an upstanding projection on a hand protector fitted to the barrels, adjusted to the eye of the shooter, a flap fixed upon a glove worn on the left hand, or a similar device on a stall worn on the left thumb. This method can only be regarded as temporary, pending adoption of one of the others. 4. Use a right-shoulder gun with sufficient cast-off for the left eye to align correctly.

Some men may shoot a little to the left all their lives, this being concealed from them by the spread of shot, which provides a margin of error. This may happen owing to too little cast-off, even to a right-eyed man. In some instances it is found necessary to cast-off a gun sufficiently to be correctly aligned for both eyes, providing what is called a "central vision" gun. But this can only be adjusted properly by the actual test of aiming and shooting at a target with both eyes open (not taking a snap shot) to ascertain if the shot strikes the object in view.

GUN FITTING.

In aligning with a shot-gun there is only one sight available and that is of a very unobtrusive kind. The front sight may be used consciously on some occasions when taking a deliberate shot, and by most people is used unconsciously to aid in aligning a moving gun. Whether observed consciously or unconsciously it serves its purpose in positioning the muzzle, but the shot-gun, unlike the rifle, has no back-sight wherewith to position the breech. It is perfectly easy to fit a back-sight to a shot-gun but very difficult indeed to use one successfully. In shooting at winged game allowances have to be given which preclude altogether the idea of aiming deliberately through two sights *at* the bird. By the time the charge got there the bird would have gone. Successful alignment can only be made on the place the bird is going to. The deliberate shot with a rifle is usually taken with the left eye closed, whereas the user of a shot-gun should keep both eyes wide open, to make the best possible use of our two-eyed system of vision. To ensure that the barrels shall be centred below an imaginary line from the shooter's eye to the mark (usually a spot in space towards which a bird is flying) is accordingly to be accounted as one of the purposes, and not the least important purpose, served by skilful gun fitting.

Having so far cleared the ground, let us see briefly what these purposes really are. First of all, the length of the stock requires to be so proportioned that the gun comes up easily and comfortably to bed the butt against the shoulder, with the right hand on the stock, and the left extended beneath the barrels. It is, of course, perfectly true that the right arm, bent at the elbow and brought in, could be straightened and extended forward as far as the left arm. It sounds absurd, when put in that way, to say that a short-armed man with a long-stocked gun cannot " reach the triggers." He can reach them, and if sufficiently adaptable and experienced, may even manage to shoot effectively with a gun too long in the stock. Boots too long for him would not prevent his walking, any more than a stock too long would prevent his shooting, but in neither case would a misfit be tolerated if it could be avoided. The length of stock must be properly adjusted to the physical conformation of the individual user of the gun, and that length needs to be determined with accuracy. The next purpose of the gun-fitter is to see that the butt is so shaped as to fit the shoulder of the shooter.

With the gun at his shoulder the shooter cannot see the stock. It may be that the heel sticks up so as to be visible to anyone standing behind, though the shooter himself knows nothing about it. Alternatively, the toe may go too low beneath the shoulder. In either case the rounded butt is not bedded where it ought to be, recoil may bruise the muscles, and the alignment of the barrels is altered. Here again allowances can be made for a misfit. It is quite possible for an experienced trick shot to make allowances even for holding his gun wrong side up, but why should any man who shoots for pleasure submit to the discomfort of an ill-fitting gun ? When the gun is mounted its butt should automatically bed itself on the shoulder, not above it nor below, neither requiring adjustment to get the stock properly home, nor necessitating allowances because it does not fit.

The more intricate problem for the gun-fitter is that of ensuring, when both hands are in position and the stock properly at the shoulder, that the barrels shall align correctly to the guidance of the aiming eye. In rifle shooting the back-sight and the fore-sight together simplify the task. The shotgun, with no back-sight at all and not very much of a fore-sight, calls for different treatment. Probably the aiming eye, to a certain extent, perceives something of connection between the breech of the gun and the front sight, but is focussed, not on the near gun, but on the distant game. The barrels in effect, act as a pointer, with this difference, that not only the tip of the pointer but its whole length must be in alignment with the object pointed at. The way to accomplish this is to ensure that the aiming eye shall be positioned naturally over the top rib of the gun. Assuming the right eye to be the master-eye, it is obvious that the right shoulder, on which the stock is bedded, lies a good deal further to the right than the eye does. For this reason what is known as " cast-off " is provided, the stock being slightly bent out to the right, so that when the cheek is brought down to the face of the stock, the barrels, out in front, come in, as it were, to meet the eye.

Cast-off should be given to all guns intended to be used from the right shoulder ; cast-on for all guns to be used from the left shoulder. A gunmaker must make a study of this important feature in gunmaking, or he can never be a perfect " fitter." Unless a gun, to be used from right shoulder and right eye, is cast-off sufficiently for the build of the man who is to use it (it may only be one-eighth of an inch, or it may be as much as or more than five-eighths) it will lie across the body— *i.e.*, point to the left and shoot to the left. So also will it shoot to the left if the stock is so long that the gun mounts on the arm instead of the pectoral muscle. This may be corrected sometimes by laying the head over to the right, but that is a move after the gun has been put to the shoulder, and is fatal to good shooting.

When the left eye is the " master-eye " and the gun is used from the left shoulder, " cast-on " serves the same purpose as " cast-off " does in the normal case of right-eyed shooting. To a left-eyed man who shoots from the right shoulder two courses are open. The first is either to close the left eye, or otherwise screen it from the gun barrels, but this is a serious handicap, throwing as it does, all the work upon one eye, and that the weaker of the two.   The alternative is to use an "across-eyed" gun, which is one built to fit the right shoulder but cast-off sufficiently to allow the rib of the barrels to come opposite the left eye for the alignment.

During his long experience of coaching and fitting, the author became convinced that through peculiarities of vision a man may unconsciously become very dangerous at the covert side where cover is thick.   He may, as he thinks, be shooting between two trees, whereas his faulty sight causes him really to point the gun more to the left-hand one, and with a tree having smooth bark, the shot is liable to *ricochet* from it to his next hand " gun," who may unfortunately receive some of the glancing pellets in his face, or perhaps lose an eye.   The offender will all the while protest that such a result is impossible, because he shot at an object a good deal to the right of the tree or *vice versa*, should he be a left-handed shot ; but it is nevertheless a fact.   If any one doubts the truth of this assertion, let him cover up or shut the right eye, keep the head fairly erect, and take a snap shot at a mark on a white-washed wall, and see where the shot will go ; or let him make the experiment when standing in front of a looking-glass, and he will find the muzzles of the barrels pointing away to the left.   In other words, he will find the left eye, and the bead on the barrels, aligned a long way to the left side of his face, as reflected accurately by the glass.

C

B

T

An "across-eyed" gun

GUN MEASUREMENTS.

When it is desired to take the measurements of an existing gun, the following method is recommended, if the appliances used for the purpose by gunmakers are not available.

A perfectly straight lath of wood, about the length of the gun, should be placed on edge along the groove of the rib and secured by tying it to the barrels. The lath then extends right to the extremity of the stock, which slants away beneath it. The gun should then be laid on its side on the table, and the following dimensions should be carefully taken to sixteenths of an inch: From Y to C and from Z to B to give the bend of the stock. From X to H, X to M, and X to T give the length of the stock, measurements being taken from the front trigger, X, with the safety slide forward.

The cast-off or -on is the distance of the points C, B and T from the vertical plane through the axis of the barrels (*see illustration*, p. 131). Measurements of this kind cannot very well be taken with home-made appliances. In cases where really accurate dimensions cannot be ascertained, a normal " cast-off " may be assumed to exist, and the amount of it may safely be left to the gunmaker.

SHOOTING SCHOOLS.

Much has been said and written of Shooting Schools and the useful purpose they serve, but strange to say, they are not yet regarded as being so essential to the shooter as the Schools that propound the science of other sports to their prospective aspirants.

Perhaps this is not so surprising after all, because there was a time, not long distant, when many an experienced shot knew as much about shooting as did the Instructor.

The experience gained by the Instructor since the days when Shooting Schools were in their infancy is now being used to the advantage of the present day sportsmen.

It was only quite natural that the Instructor of earlier days should have experienced frequent failures, and it was through these failures that he became intimate with the difficulties his pupils encountered, and they caused him to make a close study of some difficulties which were not only non-existent in his own shooting but invisible in the shooting of others, to any except those with a highly trained eye and a long daily experience covering many years.

The science of shooting is advancing but very slowly, largely because there are so few Shooting Schools to advance it. It is quite true that there are very many good shots in all four corners of the earth ; but no living soul, no matter how well he himself can shoot, can qualify with this solitary endowment to instruct a community of shooters with individual character-istics and a deeply seated instinct to do the wrong thing.

In the same way, a doctor could not qualify for his profession were he to confine his study to the diagnosis of the maladies from which he himself may have suffered. He must, among other things, come into daily contact with and study the maladies of others, not merely for a few weeks each year, but daily for many years, before he can qualify.

This is the case of the Shooting Instructor of to-day. He has pupils through his hands daily, and after years of study, both at his School and in the field, he is able to recognise certain symptoms as being prejudicial to the pupil and prescribes accordingly.

It is true that some cases are " fatal," but this is often due to the pupil not taking the " medicine."

In no other sport does custom treat the tyro so unfairly as in the subject of Shotgun Shooting. Practically all public schools have their coaches for the various games played there ; whilst the science of Golf is being expounded by professionals on many thousands of golf courses, and even the sister sport of Rifle shooting, which, although it is not so intricate an art as Game-shooting, is catered for by a large number of clubs all over the country. Therefore, game-shooting, being, as it is, so pregnant with difficulties and pursued with a death-dealing weapon, should be practised first of all at a Shooting School.

To explain what a modern Shooting School does for its various visitors would require a volume to itself. It can do as much for the experienced shot who has developed many bad habits as it can for the pupil who has not commenced shooting.

For the boy it can do much. . He is taught a few simple rules of the " Art of Shooting " which form a foundation for his shooting still to come. First of all, he is taught how to open, load and close a gun ; to see that it is always unloaded except when actually expecting a shot ; how to carry a gun to the safety of others and comfort of himself ; how to hold the gun, though unloaded, when talking to members of the party between drives ; and many other things that will minimise the possibility of those dreadful accidents one frequently hears of.

It is not necessary to describe the various appliances used at these Schools as they are only a means to an end, and to aid this end, clay pigeons are thrown by machines, sometimes singly, sometimes in coveys, at every conceivable angle.

When reference to clay pigeons is made, it is sometimes said that they start quickly and lose pace, whereas a bird starts slowly and gains pace, and in consequence they are not considered good practice. At first thought this appears to be so, but on further consideration it is not the case.

First of all, a bird does not get up slowly, but on the contrary gets up very quickly and soon attains its maximum speed, and is, therefore, not by any means always increasing its speed when fired at.

Furthermore, in the case of birds driven over a long distance, they are sometimes slightly slackening their speed ; especially so in the case of grouse in the early part of the season.

When this is considered, with the fact that no competent Instructor will teach his pupil to hit the clay pigeon except when it is travelling at a fast rate, and before the slackening of speed is perceptible, the gulf between the flight of a clay and the live bird is not so great after all.

Independent of these comparisons, the modern Shooting School with the aid of the clay pigeon is able to teach a style of shooting that incorporates the task of killing one's quarry in a manner that produces the least possible chance of firing in a line dangerous to others.

It must not be forgotten that the unpardonable act of firing down the line when driving is usually caused by not " picking up " the bird in the proper manner at the right moment. Surely the most biased mind will not deny that for this reason, if for no other, the clay pigeon serves an admirable purpose for demonstration and development of style.

It is quite natural, owing to the recurring accidents in the field, that there should be a growing custom of judging shooters, not by their ability to kill birds, but by their ability to shoot at them in a manner safe to others.

A safe shot is usually a good one, and even when he shoots badly his style is pleasing to watch ; a style that bears a striking similarity in all those who employ it, and which impresses us with a deep feeling of confidence and security for our own safety.

The very simplicity of this style at first rendered diagnosis extremely difficult, but after many years of study, the Shooting School is now able to do much for those who are desirous of acquiring a graceful style and one enabling them to shoot safely and well, and for the foregoing reasons should be given a greater amount of support.

CARTRIDGES.

Although the shotgun cartridge as we know it today is a comparatively recent production, the history of the hand firearm which could be carried and fired by one man is a long one. Early specimens were rifles in the sense that, although smooth-bore, they fired a single projectile. Reference to them here is made solely because it is from them that we have derived the system of shotgun nomenclature. A barrel of such an internal size that a close-fitting spherical ball of pure lead weighed one-twelfth of a pound became known as a 12 bore and the guns named in similar fashion range from the mighty 4 bore to the diminutive 32.

The two distinct eras of the shotgun are the muzzle-loading and the breech-loading. Included in the first is the match-lock, in which pressure on the trigger brought the lighted match back on to the pan, the cover of which had previously been pushed aside. Then came the wheel-lock in which the " wheel " was wound up with a spanner against the tension of a powerful V mainspring. After priming, the pan cover was pushed back and the limb holding the pyrites lowered to rest on it. Release of the spring forced the cover forward and the pyrites came in contact with the serrations in the rim of the rapidly rotating wheel, causing sparks to fall on the priming. This type was followed by the flint-lock, in which the flint in the jaws of the " cock " fell upon the steel " hammer " and sparks were directed down into the pan. These three types had it in common that the flash from the priming in the pan was conveyed through the touch hole to the main powder charge inside the barrel. The means of ignition were thus an integral part of the gun and this was still the case in the percussion gun which eventually evolved from the researches of the Rev. Alexander Forsyth into the behaviour of fulminate of mercury. The percussion cap was placed over a nipple with a hole leading forward and down direct to the powder charge but here was at last a system of ignition lending itself to incorporation in a cartridge for use in a breech-loading gun with drop-down barrels.

The date when a charge of small shot was first used to shoot game will probably never be known, but the gradual acceptance of this usage led to a code, probably unwritten, comprising the loads of powder and shot which experience had shown to be the most suitable for each of the commonly used bores of gun. When cartridges came into use the inside diameter naturally had to be the same as that of the barrel, and, equally, the space required for the accepted charge determined the length of the case. The internal diameter of the barrel near the breech had, however, to be increased because of the thickness of the case, or, in other words, chambering as we know it became necessary. The dimensions and means of ignition having thus been fixed over a century ago what has happened since has been development and refinement.

In the pin-fire a brass pin projected radially from the base of the case and when struck it fired a cap positioned internally. Lancaster followed very shortly with his base-fire cartridge which incorporated something similar to the paper cap used in the toy pistols of our youth placed between the base of the cartridge and an inner metal plate perforated with four flash holes. The invention was in its turn as momentous as the introduction of the percussion system and the breech-loader, as we see in it the first true and practical centre fire cartridge, and it antedated by several years the cartridge as we now know it with the percussion cap sunk centrally in the base with an internal anvil taking the place of the nipple. This type is attributed to Schneider and/or Pottet and was not introduced here until 1861 by Daw of London. From then on there has been no change in the principle of the case, although striving for perfection led to many variations in detail and quality. These have led back to two types only, the deep brass and the shallow brass, both of which are given a comparatively high degree of resistance to water by dipping into a solution of suitable properties the exposed paper of the loaded cartridge.

The last years of the nineteenth century saw the appearance of many types of smokeless powders and the black powder which for so long had been the only propellant has now virtually disappeared. Smokeless powders differed from each other and from black powder in many ways but nearly all had the common property that the correct load occupied the same space in the cartridge as the corresponding load of black powder. They were thus known as bulk powders, although the weight of the load was quite different. Bulking was an expensive process in the production of the old powders such as Smokeless Diamond and E. C. which served us well for so long, in spite of the fact that they were inclined to be affected by changes in atmospheric conditions. Moreover, they were based on cotton which had to be imported and paid for in dollars, so extinction of them became economically inevitable. The new powders developed by Messrs. Imperial Chemical Industries, Ltd., are designed to have the same ballistic attributes but they are condensed powders of which neither the weight nor the volume corresponds to black powder. To speak of a powder charge as being a " 3 dr. equivalent " is not very revealing and may even be misleading. These powders are much more stable and the burning rate will remain constant under all reasonable conditions of storage. This means that the ballistic level given by cartridges loaded with the new powders will always be close to that decided upon by the cartridge loader, as the behaviour of the cartridges in the field will be less affected by weather conditions.

The shooter of muzzle-loading days found that turning his old hats into fairly efficient wadding was a convenient way of disposing of them and it was but natural that felt should have been the most commonly used material for many years. It was, however, never very cheap and variations in quality and hardness affected the efficiency with which it sealed the bore in front of the powder gases. Air, however, does behave consistently under pressure so it is not surprising that the air cushion type of wadding is now very widely used. In this, compression of a column of air forces the comparatively thin paper tube surrounding it into close contact with the inside of the barrel, making the wad one of the most efficient obturators used in shotgun ammunition today.

For a very long time there has been no change in the leavening of lead with arsenic and antimony to give it the requisite properties for use as shot nor in the means of production by the dropping of molten globules down a tower into water. Elimination of many of the sizes formerly made has still left an ample variety for all purposes and the standard $1\frac{1}{8}$ oz. shot load of black powder days was long ago reduced to $1\frac{1}{16}$ oz. Acceptance of 1 oz. or even less as the standard is likely to follow the introduction in recent years of the crimped cartridge in which this method of closure replaces the old over-shot top wad held in place by a rolled turnover. This type improves the performance of an individual barrel so that 1 oz. shot gives the same patterns as $1\frac{1}{16}$ oz. in a turnover cartridge with, of course, a reduction in recoil owing to the lighter load. Elimination of the top wad seems also to have led to elimination of the blown patterns which cause those unaccountable misses so difficult to explain to our companions in the field ! It seems likely that in a few years the advantages of crimped closure will have made this cartridge the universal one.

Condensed powders with less shot allow of the production of shorter cartridges occupying less space and weighing less in the pocket or bag. In the other direction, it is possible to produce a cartridge of normal length with a heavier shot charge than standard, so that for the time being a gun is converted into the equivalent of one taking a longer cartridge, though with heavier recoil. This is, of course, a matter which involves the makers in the greatest care in the selection of suitable loads so that the pressure is not increased beyond what is safe. It cannot be too strongly emphasised that the pressure produced is the vital point in the conjunction of gun and cartridge. Recognition of this is readily to be seen in the new Rules of Proof, wherein the Proof markings on a gun no longer specify the maximum shot load but the service pressure for which the gun is intended.

Criticisms are sometimes heard concerning the alleged high prices of cartridges and a few words may perhaps enable the matter to be viewed in its true perspective. When it is realised that the production of a cartridge involves a very large number of operations, requiring expensive machines and skilled labour, it must remain one of the marvels of science and industry that the finished article costs less than one cheerfully pays for a simple thing such as a collar stud.

Having bought your cartridges, do not blame them if you miss an easy shot. It is a well-known fact that even the best shots sometimes have a day when eye, brain and hand are not acting in unison. Remember also that cartridges should never be subjected to extremes of temperature and humidity. Therefore do not keep your supply of them in an outhouse or near the kitchen boiler. The most suitable conditions are those that would be adopted for the preservation of leather-bound books.

The Postal Regulations forbid the sending of cartridges by post.

WEIGHT OF POWDER CHARGES.

27·334 Grains = 1 Drachm.   1 Grain = 0·0648 Gramme.

ENGLISH.   METRIC.

Grains.	Drachms.	Grammes.
1·	—	·06
6·83	¼	·44
10·	—	·64
13·67	½	·88
15·	—	·97
20·	—	1·29
20·5	¾	1·33
25·	—	1·62
27·33	1	1·77
28·	—	1·81
30·	—	1·95
33·	—	2·14
34·16	1¼	2·21
35·	—	2·27
36·	—	2·33
38·	—	2·46
40·	—	2·59
41·02	1½	2·65
42·	—	2·72
43·	—	2·78
44·	—	2·85
45·	—	2·91
47·83	1¾	3·10
50·	—	3·24
54·67	2	3·54
60·	—	3·89
61·50	2¼	3·99
68·33	2½	4·43
75·16	2¾	4·87
82·	3	5·31

WEIGHT OF SHOT CHARGES.

16 Drachms (437½ Grains) = 1 Ounce.   1 Ounce = 28·35 Grammes.

ENGLISH.   METRIC.

Ounces.	Grains.	Grammes.
1/16	27·3	1·8
1/8	54·7	3·5
1/4	109·3	7·1
1/2	218·7	14·2
3/4	328·1	21·2
1	437·5	28·3
1 1/16	464·8	30·1
1 1/8	492·2	31·9

SHOT—LETTERED SIZES.

Size.	Pellets per oz.	Size.	Pellets per oz.
L.G.	6	* S.S.S.S.S.G.	30
* M.G.	7	A.A.A.	35
S.G.	8	* A.A.	40
Special S.G.	11	* A.	50
S.S.G.	15	* B.B.B.	60
* S.S.S.G.	20	B.B.	70
* S.S.S.S.G.	25	* B.	80

SHOT—NUMBERED SIZES.

Size.	Pellets per oz.	Size.	Pellets per oz.
1	100	* 6½	300
*2	120	7	340
3	140	8	450
4	170	9	580
*4½	200	*10	850
5	220	*11	1,040
*5½ (Medium Game) ...	240	*12	1,250
6	270	*Dust	2,600

These are the British sizes. Those used in other countries vary considerably.

*These sizes are no longer made, but, as a matter of interest, they have been retained in these and following tables.

NUMBER OF PELLETS TO CHARGE.

Size.	¾ oz.	⅞ oz.	1 oz.	1 1/16 oz.	1⅛ oz.	1¼ oz.
4	128	148	170	181	191	213
4½	150	175	200	212	225	250
5	165	192	220	234	248	275
5½	180	210	240	255	270	300
6	202	236	270	287	304	338
6½	225	262	300	319	338	375
7	255	298	340	361	383	425
8	338	394	450	478	506	562

STANDARD SHOT LOADS USED IN I.C.I. PROPRIETARY
CARTRIDGES

Bore	Gun chamber length	Shot load	Brand
	in.	oz.	
4	4	3	" 4 Gauge "
8	$3\frac{1}{4}$	2	" 8 Gauge "
10	$2\frac{7}{8}$	$1\frac{7}{16}$	" 10 Gauge "
10	$2\frac{5}{8}$	$1\frac{5}{16}$	" 10 Gauge "
12	3	$1\frac{3}{8}$	" Alphamax "
12	$2\frac{3}{4}$	$1\frac{1}{4}$	" Alphamax "
12	$2\frac{1}{2}$	$1\frac{3}{16}$	" Maximum "
12	$2\frac{1}{2}$	$1\frac{1}{8}$ or $1\frac{1}{16}$	" Grand Prix " etc.
12	$2\frac{1}{2}$	1	" Impax "
12	2	$\frac{7}{8}$	" Two Inch "
16	$2\frac{3}{4}$	$1\frac{1}{8}$	" Alphamax "
16	$2\frac{1}{2}$	$\frac{15}{16}$	" Grand Prix "
20	$2\frac{3}{4}$	1	" Alphamax "
20	$2\frac{1}{2}$	$\frac{13}{16}$	" Twenty Gauge "
28	$2\frac{1}{2}$	$\frac{9}{16}$	" Grand Prix "
.410	$2\frac{1}{2}$	$\frac{7}{16}$	" Fourlong "
.410	2	$\frac{5}{16}$	" Fourten "

RANGES IN YARDS AND METRES.

Yards.	Metres.	Yards.	Metres.
1	·91	15	13·72
2	1·83	20	18·29
3	2·74	25	22·86
4	3·66	30	27·43
5	4·57	35	32·00
10	9·14	40	36·58

TIME ALONG RANGE.

FOR FLIGHT OF SHOT FROM MUZZLE TO OBJECT FOR STANDARD GAME
CARTRIDGES.

SIZE OF SHOT.	RANGE IN YARDS.					
	20	30	35	40	45	50
	sec.	sec.	sec.	sec.	sec.	sec.
3	·0560	·0910	·1103	·1306	·1529	·1767
4	·0560	·0917	·1114	·1326	·1552	·1801
5	·0560	·0923	·1125	·1346	·1584	·1844
5½	·0560	·0925	·1129	·1352	·1594	·1859
6	·0560	·0928	·1135	·1363	·1612	·1882
6½	·0560	·0932	·1142	·1373	·1628	·1906
7	·0560	·0936	·1151	·1387	·1647	·1934

MEAN VELOCITY OVER RANGE.

IN FEET-PER-SEC. FROM GUN TO OBJECT FOR STANDARD GAME
CARTRIDGES.

SIZE OF SHOT.	RANGE IN YARDS.					
	20	30	35	40	45	50
3	1,070	989	953	919	883	849
4	1,070	981	942	905	869	833
5	1,070	975	933	892	853	814
5½	1,070	972	929	887	847	807
6	1,070	969	925	880	837	796
6½	1,070	965	919	874	830	787
7	1,070	961	912	865	819	775

DIAMETER OF SPREAD.

Being the diameter in inches covered by the whole charge of a gun at various ranges for all calibres.

BORING OF GUN.	RANGE IN YARDS.						
	10	15	20	25	30	35	40
True Cylinder	20	26	32	38	44	51	57
Improved Cylinder ...	15	20	26	32	38	44	51
Quarter Choke	13	18	23	29	35	41	48
Half Choke	12	16	21	26	32	38	45
Three-quarter Choke ...	10	14	18	23	29	35	42
Full Choke	9	12	16	21	27	33	40

PATTERNS AT ALL RANGES.

The following table gives the percentage of total pellets in the 30-inch circle for six borings of gun at the ranges stated. With this information and knowing the total number of pellets in the charge, it is possible to calculate the number of pellets in the 30-inch circle for any shot charge at the ranges given.

Range	True Cylinder percentage	Improved Cylinder percentage	Quarter Choke percentage	Half Choke percentage	Three-quarter Choke percentage	Full Choke percentage
30 yds.	60	72	77	83	91	100
35 yds.	49	60	65	71	77	84
40 yds.	40	50	55	60	65	70
45 yds.	33	41	46	50	55	59
50 yds.	27	33	38	41	46	49
55 yds.	22	27	30	33	37	40
60 yds.	18	22	25	27	30	32

Example.—Charge $1\frac{1}{16}$ oz. No. 5, find pattern at 50 yards for a half choke barrel. Total pellets 234, multiplied by 41 (from table above) and divided by 100. Answer 95·9, say 96.

Guns are normally tested at 40 yards and the next six pages give the patterns at this distance with the above six borings. The recognised 12-bore testing load is $1\frac{1}{16}$ oz. of No. 6 shot.

TRUE CYLINDER (= 40%) PATTERNS.

Oz. of Shot	Pellets in 30 in. circle at 40 YARDS for different SIZES of Shot.						
	4	$4\frac{1}{2}$	5	$5\frac{1}{2}$	6	$6\frac{1}{2}$	7
$1\frac{1}{2}$	102	120	132	144	162	180	204
$1\frac{7}{16}$	97	115	126	138	155	172	196
$1\frac{3}{8}$	94	110	121	132	148	165	187
$1\frac{5}{16}$	89	105	116	126	142	158	178
$1\frac{1}{4}$	85	100	110	120	135	150	170
$1\frac{3}{16}$	81	95	104	114	128	142	162
$1\frac{1}{8}$	76	90	99	108	121	135	153
$1\frac{1}{16}$	72	85	94	102	115	128	144
ONE	68	80	88	96	108	120	136
$\frac{15}{16}$	64	75	82	90	101	112	128
$\frac{7}{8}$	60	70	77	84	94	105	119
$\frac{13}{16}$	55	65	72	78	87	98	110
$\frac{3}{4}$	51	60	66	72	81	90	102
$\frac{11}{16}$	47	55	60	66	74	82	94
$\frac{5}{8}$	42	50	55	60	68	75	85
$\frac{9}{16}$	38	45	50	54	61	68	76
$\frac{1}{2}$	34	40	44	48	54	60	68

IMPROVED CYLINDER (= 50%) PATTERNS.

Oz. of Shot.	Pellets in 30 in. circle at 40 YARDS for different SIZES of Shot.						
	4	4½	5	5½	6	6½	7
1½	128	150	165	180	202	225	255
1 7⁄16	122	144	158	173	194	216	245
1⅜	117	138	152	165	185	207	234
1 5⁄16	111	132	145	158	177	197	223
1¼	107	125	138	150	169	188	213
1 3⁄16	101	119	131	143	161	178	202
1⅛	96	113	124	135	152	169	192
1 1⁄16	91	107	117	128	144	160	181
ONE	85	100	110	120	135	150	170
15⁄16	80	94	103	113	127	141	160
⅞	75	88	97	105	118	132	149
13⁄16	69	82	90	98	110	122	138
¾	64	75	83	90	102	113	128
11⁄16	59	69	76	83	93	103	117
⅝	53	63	69	75	85	94	106
9⁄16	48	57	62	68	76	85	96
½	43	50	55	60	68	75	85

QUARTER CHOKE (= 55%) PATTERNS.

Oz. of Shot.	Pellets in 30 in. circle at 40 YARDS for different SIZES of Shot.						
	4	4½	5	5½	6	6½	7
1½	140	165	181	198	222	247	280
1 7/16	134	158	174	190	214	237	269
1 3/8	128	151	167	181	204	227	257
1 5/16	122	145	159	173	194	216	245
1¼	117	137	151	165	186	206	234
1 3/16	111	130	144	157	177	196	222
1⅛	105	124	136	148	167	186	211
1 1/16	100	117	129	140	158	175	199
ONE	93	110	121	132	148	165	187
15/16	87	103	113	124	139	155	175
7/8	82	96	106	115	130	145	164
13/16	76	90	99	107	120	134	152
3/4	70	82	90	99	111	123	140
11/16	64	75	83	90	102	113	128
5/8	58	68	75	82	93	103	117
9/16	52	62	68	74	83	93	105
½	46	55	60	67	74	82	93

HALF CHOKE (= 60%) PATTERNS.

Oz. of Shot.	Pellets in 30 in. circle at 40 YARDS for different SIZES of Shot.						
	4	4½	5	5½	6	6½	7
1½	153	180	198	216	243	270	306
1 7/16	146	173	190	207	234	259	293
1⅜	140	165	182	198	223	248	280
1 5/16	134	158	174	189	212	236	267
1¼	128	150	165	180	203	225	255
1 3/16	121	142	157	171	193	214	242
1⅛	115	135	148	162	182	203	230
1 1/16	109	128	140	153	172	191	217
ONE	102	120	132	144	162	180	204
15/16	95	112	124	135	152	169	191
⅞	89	105	116	126	142	158	179
13/16	83	98	108	117	131	146	166
¾	77	90	99	108	122	135	153
11/16	70	82	91	99	112	124	140
⅝	64	75	82	90	101	112	127
9/16	58	68	74	81	91	102	115
½	51	60	66	72	81	90	102

151

THREE-QUARTER CHOKE (= 65%) PATTERNS.

Oz. of Shot.	Pellets in 30 in. circle at 40 YARDS for different SIZES of Shot.						
	4	4½	5	5½	6	6½	7
1½	165	195	214	234	263	292	331
1 7/16	159	187	206	224	253	281	317
1 3/8	151	179	197	214	242	268	303
1 5/16	145	171	188	205	230	255	289
1¼	138	162	179	195	220	243	276
1 3/16	131	154	170	185	209	231	262
1⅛	124	146	161	175	198	219	249
1 1/16	118	139	152	166	187	207	235
ONE	110	130	143	156	176	195	221
15/16	103	121	134	146	164	183	207
⅞	97	114	126	136	154	171	194
13/16	90	106	117	127	142	158	179
¾	83	97	107	117	132	146	165
11/16	76	89	99	107	121	134	151
⅝	69	81	89	97	109	121	137
9/16	62	76	80	88	99	110	124
½	55	65	71	78	88	97	110

FULL CHOKE (= 70%) PATTERNS.

Oz. of Shot.	Pellets in 30 in. circle at 40 YARDS for different SIZES of Shot.						
	4	$4\frac{1}{2}$	5	$5\frac{1}{2}$	6	$6\frac{1}{2}$	7
$1\frac{1}{2}$	178	210	231	252	286	315	357
$\frac{7}{16}$	170	202	221	241	272	302	243
$1\frac{3}{8}$	163	192	212	231	260	289	328
$1\frac{5}{16}$	156	184	202	220	248	276	312
$1\frac{1}{4}$	149	175	192	210	267	263	298
$1\frac{3}{16}$	142	167	183	200	225	249	283
$1\frac{1}{8}$	134	157	174	189	213	236	268
$1\frac{1}{16}$	127	149	164	179	201	223	253
ONE	119	140	154	168	189	210	238
$\frac{15}{16}$	112	132	144	158	177	197	223
$\frac{7}{8}$	105	122	135	147	165	184	209
$\frac{13}{16}$	97	114	125	137	153	171	194
$\frac{3}{4}$	90	105	115	126	142	158	179
$\frac{11}{16}$	82	97	106	115	130	144	163
$\frac{5}{8}$	75	87	97	105	118	131	148
$\frac{9}{16}$	67	79	86	94	106	118	134
$\frac{1}{2}$	59	70	77	84	95	105	119

SHOT SIZES AND VELOCITY.

As to the size of shot for ordinary game shooting with light loads, No. 7 is the smallest size recommended. It is regarded with a good deal of favour, but some shooters, considering it too small, prefer a larger size with the disadvantage of fewer pellets. In this connection it is worth while to remember that with equal weights of shot charges and equal loads of powder the muzzle velocity should be the same irrespective of the size of shot. As velocities are chronographically measured by the breaking of wires placed at the muzzle and at some distance—usually 20 yards, but it may be 10 yards or 40 yards—beyond the muzzle, it will be understood that " muzzle velocity " itself is a calculated velocity. It cannot actually be measured, because at the muzzle no distance has yet been traversed. The difference in the " striking velocity " of larger and smaller pellets depends chiefly on their weight, which, in the case of leaden globules, necessarily determines also their diameter. Without going into the technical aspects of the matter, though these are not very intricate, it will suffice that the larger sizes retain their energy in flight for a longer time than the smaller sizes do. It follows that at longer ranges the larger sizes should still retain a sufficiency of striking force when smaller sizes would be spent. That this actually is so is best realised when big sizes of shot are used in heavy shoulder guns for wild-fowling, the longer range and greater killing power being obtained mainly through the better conservation of energy in larger pellets. As between the various sizes used for game this holds equally true, bearing always in mind that the differences in weight are relatively small. What the pellets lose on weight may be compensated for by the higher velocity obtained when an increased charge of powder propels a reduced charge of shot. From No. 4 to No. 8, there is an ample graduation providing opportunities for the satisfaction of individual preferences. The simple point in all cases to be borne in mind is that for equal weight of charge the choice lies between more pellets each of less weight, or fewer pellets each of greater weight, for one cannot have it both ways.

STRIKING VELOCITY.

IN FEET-PER-SEC. AT VARIOUS RANGES FOR STANDARD GAME CARTRIDGES.

SIZE OF SHOT.	RANGE IN YARDS.					
	20	30	35	40	45	50
3	915	804	753	704	657	612
4	906	788	735	683	635	587
5	893	768	711	656	604	555
5½	889	762	703	647	594	544
6	883	752	691	634	579	528
6½	878	742	681	622	566	513
7	871	731	667	606	549	496

STRIKING ENERGY.

IN FOOT-POUNDS AT VARIOUS RANGES FOR INDIVIDUAL PELLETS OF STANDARD GAME CARTRIDGES.

SIZE OF SHOT.	RANGE IN YARDS.					
	20	30	35	40	45	50
3	5·79	4·48	3·92	3·43	2·99	2·59
4	4·68	3·54	3·08	2·66	2·30	1·97
5	3·52	2·60	2·23	1·90	1·61	1·36
6	2·80	2·03	1·71	1·44	1·20	1·01
7	2·16	1·52	1·27	1·06	0·86	0·70

MAXIMUM EFFECTIVE RANGES.

On the subject of penetration little need here be said, for, within ordinary game shooting ranges, the differences as between one size of shot and another, though always appreciable, and increasing as the range lengthens, do not call for further comment than has already been made.

The table following shows the ranges at which various sizes of shot pellets lose their killing power at normal velocities. These ranges are calculated on a minimum effective striking energy of ·85 ft. lbs., the figure usually taken as a standard in such calculations. The figure may vary on either side to about ·5 ft. lbs. for snipe and similar small birds and up to 1·5 ft. lbs. for geese, etc.

Size of Shot.	Yards.	Size of Shot.	Yards.
BBB	138·4	4½	67·6
BB	127·2	5	63·2
B	118·0	5½	59·6
1	104·1	6	54·7
2	93·5	6½	50·5
3	85·1	7	45·8
4	75·2	8	36·1

Note that these ranges are the maxima for *individual* shot pellets; pattern density has an equally important effect on the effective range of a whole shot charge. Variations in gun boring, shot loads and shot sizes make it difficult to lay down figures for pattern density; the only hint possible here is that, with all but the smallest sizes of shot or the heaviest shot loads from special large-bore wildfowling guns, pattern density fails long before pellet energy.

KILLS TO CARTRIDGES.

This is a matter often discussed. In a previous edition
an extract was given from the *Badminton Magazine* summarising
a correspondence in which Lord Walsingham's average of 30
per cent., as a fair proportion for a good shot, was taken
exception to. Lord Walsingham's exact words were:—

" Sixty in a hundred is good shooting throughout any day
but thirty is nearer the mark with most good shots if you take
the season through, allowing for a fair proportion of wild game."

An average of 50 per cent., or even more, if all the shooting is
easy, may very well represent a much lower grade of skill than
an average of 30 per cent. where most of the shooting is difficult.
Further, a very high average of kills to cartridges may be
obtained by picking shots, just as a very low one may result
from the unsportsmanlike practice of taking chances not good
enough to take. The greater likelihood that an " impossible "
bird may get away wounded, if it does not escape untouched,
than that a lucky pellet will bring it to bag, is perhaps the
best recommendation there is for keeping an eye on " averages."
Misjudgment in firing at excessive ranges, for example, is
certain to reduce the proportion of kills to cartridges, but if
that consideration should lead the shooter to refuse chances he
ought to take, by far the best plan is to ignore altogether what
must at best be an artificial and often misleading standard.
Averages take no account of the difference between the birds
of the early and later months. As between the members of a
party all shooting at the same time and under similar conditions,
kills to cartridges may form a good criterion of relative skill,
but, for anything more, percentages are fallible guides, and
little to be relied on and perhaps this branch of arithmetic is a
little out of place in the field.

THE VELOCITY OF FLIGHT OF BIRDS.

Attempts to determine the speed at which game birds fly
have established a rule of averages, to which the individual
bird in flight is usually an exception. The speed at which men
walk is estimated, not inaccurately, at four miles an hour.
A man in a hurry may walk faster, and most men at most times
walk more slowly than that. Stepping out from milestone to
milestone a quarter of an hour to the mile represents satisfactory
going. The rule is a good rule, although to the ordinary person
taking a walk it may not apply. It is the same with the flight
of birds. The game shooter is interested to know what is the
average speed of partridges, pheasants, snipe, woodcock or
duck when on the wing. To utilise the knowledge practically
he would need to know, not what the average velocity of flight
say of pheasants, or of some particular species of the *Phasianus*,
ought to be, but what the velocity of each particular specimen,
then and there before his gun, actually is.

The late Sir R. Payne-Gallwey held that the speed of all flying game,
large or small, is " very similar." He says, in " Letters to Young
Shooters " : " I find a cock pheasant that has been fired at—not to kill,
but to alarm—will fly time after time, on a calm day, at the rate of
55 ft. to 65 ft. per second." Sixty feet being taken as an average, this
represents a convenient figure of 40 miles an hour. The late Mr. W. B.
Tegetmeier, averaging the results of a number of pigeon races found that
the rate of flight of the fastest trained homing pigeons averaged " under
40 miles an hour, and that even with a favourable wind it does not
reach 60."

On these grounds, broadly confirmed by the experiments of the late
Mr. R. W. S. Griffith, it has become usual to estimate for all game birds
a standard velocity of flight of 40 miles an hour. This, though probably
inaccurate if applied to individual birds, may very well represent an
average approximately correct. It is, of course, a common impression
that small birds fly faster than large birds. In a similar way all birds

seem to fly very much faster when near the observer than they do when at a distance. Appearances are proverbially deceptive, and these points may be considered when dealing in the next section with some aspects of aim and allowance. Meanwhile the following article, though it appeared in the *Field* so long ago as February 19th, 1887, continues to be of practical interest as giving definite details of chronographic experiments carried out with partridges and pheasants, as well as pigeons, when neither aided nor retarded by the wind.

EXPERIMENTS TO ASCERTAIN THE VELOCITY OF FLIGHT OF BIRDS.

The rate of speed attained by birds that are commonly shot by sportsmen has been the subject of a good deal of discussion in the *Field*, and very conflicting opinions have been expressed with respect to their powers of flight. In order, if possible, to obtain data of a more reliable character than many vague surmises which have been indulged in, we requested the assistance of Mr. Griffith, who has from time to time furnished our readers with so much valuable information relative to the velocities of shot and the explosive force of gunpowders ; and he not only very kindly complied with our request, but has improved upon the method we suggested for carrying out the experiments.

The series of trials was commenced with pigeons, which it was thought might probably be more amenable than wild game to the conditions connected with their flight, and so, in the event of there being any hitch in the arrangements, there would be a better chance for the apparatus to be got into thorough working order before attempting experiments with partridges or pheasants. In order to secure a good standard of comparison, Mr. Hammond, the well-known purveyor of pigeons for the Hurlingham Club, was asked to select some of his very best " blue rocks " to pass through the ordeal. The experiments with these birds were carried out about two months ago, on a fine clear day in the middle of December, when there was no wind whatever to enhance or diminish the natural speed of the birds.

The pigeons commenced their flight at one end of the covered range, or experimental shooting gallery, of the Schultze Gunpowder Company, in the New Forest, and the birds thus had the opportunity of getting well on the wing before they reached the other extremity, where was placed the apparatus employed to record their rate of speed after they had flown 40 yards. Two " screens," or arrangements of fine threads, were here put into connection with the electric apparatus, and through these threads the birds must necessarily dash in their flight, in order to make their exit from the range. The so-called " screens " were composed of the finest invisible-grey cotton, so easily broken as not to check the flight of the birds in the slightest degree, and the successive breakages were instantaneously recorded by the electrical apparatus. Between the two screens there was an intervening space of 6 ft. 9 in. (a distance which was adopted for its being convenient for regulating the chrono-graph), and, the apparatus having recorded the time taken by the bird in traversing this $2\frac{1}{4}$ yards interval, the velocity was then readily convertible into yards per second or miles per hour.

In order that the birds might fly directly towards these screens, all apertures in the building were darkened except the open end of the range ; and, as the birds, on being liberated, would naturally fly towards the broad daylight, and be likely to gain full confidence as they approached the place of exit, it was hoped that each of them might be led to do its best by the time it reached the point where the record of speed was to be made. The results, on the whole, were very satisfactory. Now and then a bird would not fly straight, or would check its flight before dashing through the screens ; but whenever such was the case, the record was rejected as defective, and accordingly does not figure in the list which is given below. The number of good flights, however, was sufficient to enable Mr. Griffith to make 12 fair records of speed, the particulars of which are as follows :—

PIGEONS IN THE 40 YARDS' RANGE	TIME. Seconds.	RATE OF SPEED.	
		Yards. per Second.	Miles. per Hour.
1st	·157	14·3	29·3
2nd	·156	14·4	29·5
3rd	·168	13·4	27·4
4th	·150	15·0	30·7
5th	·163	13·8	28·2
6th	·139	16·2	33·1
7th	·169	13·3	27·2
8th	·153	14·7	30·1
9th	·168	13·4	27·4
10th	·176	12·8	26·1
11th	·157	14·3	29·3
12th	·136	16·5	33·8

Having obtained the above chronographic results in the covered range, Mr. Griffith was not content to let matters end there, and he therefore determined to place these velocities in comparison with records of flight in the open. For this purpose he adopted a method very similar to that which has since been suggested by " Vivarii Custos " (*Field*, Jan. 15) as a means of ascertaining the flight of driven partridges. Mr. Griffith placed men in ambush at various measured distances, with instructions to signal as soon as a bird arrived opposite either of the stations. When the bird had flown 25 yards from the starting point in the open the time was taken by means of a stop watch, and the record was completed as soon as the signal was given of the bird having accomplished either of the measured distances. In four instances the birds went straight away, and the records were as under :—

FLIGHT OF PIGEONS. IN THE OPEN.	TIME. Seconds.	RATE OF SPEED.	
		Yards per Second.	Miles. per Hour.
240 yards	19	.... 12·6	.... 25·8
265 ,, ...	20	.... 13·2	.... 27·0
300 ,, ...	22	.... 13·6	.... 27·9
132 ,, ...	10	.... 13·2	.... 27·0

With reference to these results Mr. Griffith says : " I expected the free long flight would beat the chronograph velocities at 40 yards, but the reverse is the case. I imagine the reason is, that when started from a trap or basket, as these were, the birds fly in alarm at first, but when away in the open they do not keep up their full pace." In neither case, however, did these " blue rocks " come up to the average speed of the trained " homing birds " of which Mr. Tegetmeier gave particulars in the *Field* of the 22nd ult. There the average speed of the winning birds in 18 pigeon races amounted to 36 miles an hour—the highest velocity, with a favourable wind, being at the rate of 55 miles an hour. In Mr. Griffith's experiments the highest velocity was nearly 34 miles an hour, without any wind whatever.

Mr. Griffith's next task was to try similar experiments with partridges and pheasants, and for that purpose it was desirable to obtain a supply of good wild birds, as those kept in confinement could not be taken as fair representatives of the power of flight of birds which had always been at liberty. The difficulty, however, for many weeks, was to get such specimens as were wanted, the snow upon the ground and other circumstances being unfavourable to their capture. At length, however, some birds were obtained, all very wild and active, and last week Mr. Griffith proceeded with his experiments.

The conditions as to screens, &c., were as previously stated. Some of the pheasants were inveterate runners and would not rise to the screens at all ; others rose fairly, but they did not all of them exhibit an equal degree of earnestness, and the best six records obtained were as follows, the first being that of a splendid bird, who went through the screens in fine style. The respective times and velocities are as follows :—

PHEASANTS IN THE 40 YARDS' RANGE.	TIME. Seconds.		RATE OF SPEED.	
			Yards per Second.	Miles per Hour.
1st	·136		16·5	33·8
2nd	·156		14·4	29·5
3rd	·186		12·1	24·7
4th	·189		11·9	24·4
5th	·225		10·0	20·5
6th	·139		16·2	33·1

Some of the birds were also timed in the open, and, as on the day of the previous experiments, there was no wind whatever. Two of the pheasants went away straight at fine speed ; a third doubled back, and is therefore omitted from the record ; and the fourth went straight away, but with much less velocity than the first two. From the following records it will be seen that, contrary to the experience with the " blue rocks," the pheasants attained their highest speed in the open :—

FLIGHT OF PHEASANTS IN THE OPEN.	TIME. Seconds.		RATE OF SPEED.	
			Yards per Second.	Miles per Hour.
265 yards	15·0		17·7	36·1
220 ,,	11·8		18·6	38·1
140 ,,	10·6		13·2	27·0

The concluding experiment was with the partridges, which went fairly well at the screens, though they did not seem to exert themselves very much ; and the following were the records obtained :—

PARTRIDGES IN THE 40 YARDS' RANGE.	TIME. Seconds.		RATE OF SPEED.	
			Yards per Second.	Miles. per Hour.
1st	·172		13·1	26·8
2nd	·188		12·0	24·5
3rd	·194		11·6	23·7
4th	·162		13·9	28·4

Here, in the range, the partridges did not fly so fast as the " blue rocks " but they did better in the open, so far as the records go. Only two of

11

them, however, flew far enough to have their time recorded. The rest dropped to the ground before they got to the men who were stationed to signal their arrival. The speeds of these two were as follows :—

FLIGHT OF PARTRIDGES IN THE OPEN.	TIME. Seconds.	RATE OF SPEED.	
		Yards per Second.	Miles per Hour.
170 yards	12·6	13·5	27·6
220 ,,	14·0	15·7	32·1

Mr. Griffith says, in conclusion: " I think the velocities may be fairly taken as the speed of birds rising to the gun, and also of driven game when not aided by any wind."

Of course, when driven birds are going down wind with all the advantage of a strong breeze, the velocity of the wind has to be added to the natural speed of the bird. In order to afford an idea of the amount of assistance that would be rendered to birds flying down wind, a short table of velocities may be given. A wind moving at the rate of three or four miles an hour is scarcely perceptible ; and other gradations in miles per hour, and feet per second, are as follows :—

	Miles per Hour.	Feet per Second.		Miles per Hour.	Feet per Second
Gentle air	7	10·25	Gale	40	58·68
Light breeze	14	20·50	Heavy storm	60	88·0
Steady breeze	21	30·75	Hurricane	80	117·36

It will be seen that a mile per hour is just about equivalent to 1½ feet per second.

THE PHYSIOLOGY OF SHOOTING.

BY WM. JAS. FLEMING, M.D.

Reprinted from the *Field*.

It is universally admitted that good shooting depends less upon the gun than upon the man behind it. The gun and all connected with it have received, and still receive, most minute and careful study, but little attention has been devoted to the human element in marksmanship. In so far as shooting goes, the man is as purely a machine as the gun, but a much more complicated and less understood piece of mechanism, and, to make the problem worse, an individual mechanism—no two quite alike. There are, however, some principles and arrangements common to every human shooting machine which can be formulated, and in this paper I will try to place them as clearly as possible before my readers. For this purpose it will only be necessary to consider the problems connected with shooting at moving objects, as this embraces all the questions arising out of target practice.

To begin with, let us try to analyse the processes which result in a bird coming down a few yards from where it rose near a good shot. First, he sees the bird—that is to say, the image of the bird is sharply focused on his retina by the proper adjustment of the internal mechanism of the eye. In this retina the picture thrown upon it sets up nervous changes, which are conveyed to some part of the brain, and there produce what we call vision—in reality, a change in some part of the nervous tissue of the brain. At the same time he judges the distance of the bird and the direction and rate of its flight by a complicated process, of which more hereafter. The information thus gained is transformed at first by an effort of will, but, after sufficient practice, automatically, into orders affecting nearly all the muscles of the body. He plants his feet firmly and raises his gun (for simplicity sake here we will suppose he is a shot who takes aim—a question afterwards to be discussed). Having raised the gun, he looks along it, and, I believe, by a continual alteration of the focus of his eye, sees both the sight and the bird at one time, and waits till they are in one line. Again this state of affairs is communicated to the brain by the eye, and an order sent to the finger to pull the trigger ; then the mechanism is all gun. It is all done in the fraction of a second, but it must all be done, and really much more.

I must now endeavour to explain the above somewhat more fully, but will take it for granted that the reader knows enough of ordinary optics to require no more detailed explanation of how the bird is seen, only remarking that it is by no means an instantaneous process.

Seeing the bird, how does he judge its distance from him ? *By the summation of the various adjustments his eyes require to make to see clearly, compared with previous experience.* The principal of these adjustments are the amount of convergence of the two eyes required to bring their optical axes to a point at the bird, and the amount of accommodation necessary to bring the image of the bird to a sharp focus on the retina. These adjustments are made by muscles both without and within the eye, and we are informed of their amount by the *muscular sense.* This muscular sense is really the keynote of the whole question, and therefore requires some further explanation.

It is not generally known that we possess a distinct power of appreciating the amount of muscular force required to perform an action, quite separate from our sense of touch. Perhaps the best way to understand this is to consider the different effects of, say, a pound weight laid upon our palm with the back of the hand resting upon the table, and the same weight lifted freely up and down, as we instinctively do in estimating weight. In the first case we feel the pressure of a cold, hard body, but, if not aided by sight, have a very faint idea of its weight ; indeed, we can scarcely tell the difference between one and two pounds if the surfaces touching the palm are of nearly the same area, and if the objects are gently deposited, the eyes being shut, and the hand motionless and supported. If, however, the weights are lifted by the arm, we at once appreciate the difference. This muscular sense plays a very important part in our lives, and is peculiarly capable of training. A good example of this is the power acquired by letter-sorters in the post office to detect by the hand alone the slightest over-weight, a practised hand rarely erring. It is by this muscular sense, telling us how much we have required to use the muscles both within and without the eye, that we estimate distance.

To return to the bird, we have seen that a series of complicated processes are necessary merely to see it and judge approximately its distance ; but, aided by experience, we learn by means of the same mechanism, and practically simultaneously, a great deal more about it—the angle in relation to our position at which it is flying, an idea of the pace it is going, &c. Having unconsciously, or at least, apparently so, got all this information, which, of course, is largely due to practice, the brain condition thus set up induces (in what physiologists call an automatic manner) a large number of muscular actions—planting the feet, raising the gun, and in the case of the man who aims, which we are now considering, closing one eye and bringing the other to a place in relation to the gun suitable for aligning the barrel with the bird ; then information is carried to the brain that the gun is " on," and an order sent to the finger to pull the trigger. In the case of the man who shoots with both eyes open and the head erect—who, in fact, does not look along the gun at all—we have a somewhat different order of proceeding. He estimates in the same way the distance, direction, and rapidity of flight ; but having done this, trusts entirely to his muscular sense to hold the gun straight and to tell him when it is straight. To succeed in this can only be the result of practice ; but we must remember that the muscular sense varies enormously in accuracy and rapidity of expression in different men, and even in the same man at different times and under different conditions. Some men hear, see, taste and smell better than others ; why should we wonder that they differ in this sense also, or that one individual requires more training or practice than another to achieve the same accuracy ?

This difference between individuals is not confined to their muscular sense, but exists in an even more marked way in the amount of time required by each to go through the complicated nervous and muscular actions which I have described. Attention was first drawn to this by the astronomers, who found that it is necessary to allow for what is called " personal error " in the observations of different individuals. For instance, suppose it is required to observe the exact moment at which a star touches a hair stretched across the field of a stationary telescope, and that by a suitable arrangement two observers are enabled to watch through the telescope at the same time— it will be found that an appreciable difference exists in the record of each. What is more, this difference will be practically constant for the same individual, constituting his " personal equation," which has to be allowed for in subsequent calculations. By modifications of this idea, physiologists have succeeded in measuring, not only the time taken by the whole process, but the time occupied by each of its component parts.

To go into the details of these experiments is needless here, but, in order to give a general idea of the methods employed, it may be well to describe one or two of them. Let us take first the one which has been perhaps best worked out—the determination of the rapidity with which an impulse travels along a nerve. If we arrange a stimulus—most conveniently an electric shock—so that when applied, let us suppose over a nerve in the forearm, it causes a contraction of the muscles of a finger, and consequently a movement of the finger, and if we measure the exact time which elapses between the electric shock and the movement of the finger, first when the stimulus is applied, say, nine inches from the finger, and again three inches from the finger, the difference will give us the time taken for transmission through the six inches, and therefore the rate.

Some of the readers of this article may be interested in the apparatus employed in making these delicate measurements, so I will briefly describe the essential features. We require a surface moving rapidly and regularly, upon which a faint motion can easily make a mark. This is generally obtained by a large cylinder rotated by clockwork, and covered with smoked paper. Upon this are inscribed, by light contact, motions, however slight, communicated to levers. For the experiment just mentioned, to determine the rapidity of transmission of nervous impulses, three of these levers would be required—one attached to the finger to be moved, one actuated by the same electric current which gives the shock, and one connected with a chronograph or instrument for marking time. This is generally a tuning fork, the number of whose vibrations is known, and of course constant. If, then, with the three levers adjusted to write exactly perpendicular to each other, the cylinder is rotated, we shall have three straight lines drawn. If, now, the tuning fork is made to vibrate, the lever attached to it will mark curves, and if, now, the electric shock is sent into the nerve, the lever connected with it will move and mark the exact moment of stimulation. As soon as the muscles of the finger begin to respond to the stimulus, the lever attached to the finger will mark, and the difference between the two, read by the vibrations of the tuning fork, which have been going on all the time, gives the time of transmisson. Our tracing then will be something like this, and the distance between the lines *a* and *a'* read on the tuning fork the actual time of

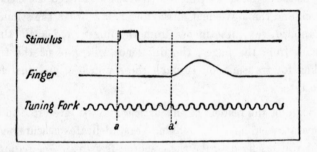

nervous transmission, less the latent period of the muscle, which we need not consider in this case. By this experiment, more or less modified, it has been calculated that the rate of transmission of motor stimuli in man is only 120 feet per second. Your readers will remember that shot at 40 yards travels at the rate of about 600 feet per second.

To estimate the time taken by the whole process, for the conversion of a visual image into a voluntary muscular action —which is exactly what takes place between seeing a bird and pulling the trigger—a slightly different arrangement is required. The person to be experimented upon is seated with his finger on an electrical key, so arranged that the moment it is depressed, a mark is recorded upon the revolving cylinder. A blue and red light are fixed so that either can be shown at the option of the experimenter. The subject of the experiment is directed only to depress the key when one of those lights is shown, and the instant at which this light is exposed is also recorded upon the cylinder. A chronograph is used as before. By this means we are able to estimate the whole time taken by both the nervous transmission and the mental judgment of which of the two lights was shown. The result of a number of experiments on these lines give for different individuals from $\frac{1}{100}$ of a second to $\frac{6}{100}$ of a second. Now, if we consider that this corresponds to the interval between the gunner seeing the bird and pulling the trigger, we can easily calculate that if the bird is crossing at the rate of 50 feet per second—practically thirty-four miles an hour—in the case of a man with $\frac{1}{100}$ of a second personal error, it will only have flown 6 inches, whereas, in the case of the man with $\frac{6}{100}$ it will have flown 3 feet. This seems largely to explain why men differ so much in the amount they borrow. The lesson is that each individual must find out the proper " borrow " for himself, as another person, with probably quite a different personal error, cannot guide him.

Another important point in connection with this matter is the influence, noticed by all observers, which food, stimulants, and sedative, have in altering the figures for each individual. The effects vary in different persons, and this goes far to account for some men shooting better before, others after, lunch, for some men being unable to shoot if they smoke, others unable to shoot if they do not. I have tried to show that each must be a law to himself, and therefore, I trust, helped some men who have failed to get good results by following the rules of their mentors.

AIMING AND "ALLOWANCE."

The first attempts to shoot moving game will quickly prove to the beginner that it is useless simply to aim the gun at a bird and fire ; in most types of shot a miss will certainly result. Why this should be so and the means of overcoming the difficulty are such important matters in successful shooting that they demand careful consideration.

Between the eye seeing the bird and the shot striking it there is a brief but important lapse of time, which we must divide into two parts. In chronological order these are what we may call the " personal " and the " mechanical " times.

The latter covers the fall of the tumbler, the ignition of the powder, the flight of the shot up the barrel and on to the bird. In flint-lock days it would have been necessary to discuss these phases separately, but with our present guns and modern British standard load cartridges it is sufficient to say that for all practical purposes these amounts may be lumped together and regarded as constant.   The time with No. 6 shot over 40 yards is about $\cdot 1419$ second.

Preceding this, however, is the " personal " time, which, as we have seen from the previous paper, varies from $\cdot 01$ to $\cdot 06$ second between individuals, depending also on the other conditions mentioned, and, it might be added, differing for the same man on different days. During the lapse of this personal time the bird has of course flown on and assuming it to be a crossing one allowance ahead obviously has to be made to ensure a hit.

In what may be described as the carry-forward method of allowance, the idea is to fire into the air at a point which the bird will reach at the same moment as the shot. Now while this may do for the man of very slight personal error, for the man of great personal error it seems impracticable because of the considerable distance it entails firing in front.

If, however, the gun, instead of being pointed in some vague direction in space, is made to cover the bird and swung to keep covering it until after the shot has been fired, we shall at once have eliminated the effects of variations in the personal time, although nothing can be done to cut out the variations themselves.

If we imagine the bird to be represented by a point on the rim of a revolving cart-wheel and the gun by a spoke pointing at it, it makes no difference when the eye and brain decide to fire, because the spoke is always correctly aligned and the personal delay in carrying out the action has no effect.

This reasoning is nearly enough correct when the spoke approximates to the 28 inches or so of a shot gun barrel but if instead we imagine a pheasant at a radius of 15 yards it is obvious that we shall have to allow for the time taken by the shot in covering the distance from the muzzle. In other words, we must now consider the "mechanical" time.

Although shot starts its flight at many times the speed of the bird, yet the latter will have covered a considerable distance after the pressing of the trigger and before the shot strikes. An allowance must therefore be made ahead to allow for this delay, and as we have already seen that by itself the great allowance often required for "personal" time makes the carry-forward method impracticable, the addition of the

" mechanical " allowance makes it even more inadvisable to attempt " intercepting."

Instead it is best to increase the " swing " mentioned above so that it not merely keeps the bird covered but gives the necessary allowance. It is important to note that the swing must not be checked either before or at the moment of firing, otherwise the shot will whistle harmlessly behind the bird's tail.

For precise information as to how much lead ought to be given at various distances the shooting world is indebted to the *Field*. To convey by the written or spoken word an idea of distance it is necessary either to cite measurements or to utilize standards of comparison, such, for instance, as the length of a pheasant. Here again the cart-wheel analogy is helpful, for the apparent length of our 15 yards pheasant would be greater than the apparent length of a 30 yards pheasant. It may be that the shooter does judge lead by the apparent length of the object he intends to hit, but written instructions show that in estimating the amount of space there ought to be, in terms of bird length, between the bird and the spot to which the shot is directed, authorities differ hopelessly. The calculations undertaken by the *Field* and published on March 19th, 1904, removed the matter out of the realms of speculation into those of fact. The full text of the article was included in a previous edition, but the following extract, now again reproduced, covers the more important points.

" In order to produce a table of allowances, for aiming at moving objects, it is necessary to adopt a characteristic rate of flight as a basis for comparison. We accordingly adopted the value of 60 ft. per second, which corresponds with 40 miles an hour, and is the average rate of flight which we have ourselves fixed by chronograph measurements for a clay bird sprung from a powerful trap and throwing at an angle with the ground more or less horizontal. It is similarly the recognised speed of a fast-flying pheasant or a driven grouse or partridge. Almost needless to say, many birds fly much slower than this, whereas others move along at a greater rate when the wind is in their favour and when the rate of flight is aided by gravity, as is the case when a bird is flushed on a hill and is inclining its course towards a lower elevation. To obtain the distance covered in a given time by a bird travelling at 60 ft. per second is a very simple matter. . . . . Without further preface, we will introduce our table, which shows the exact distance a bird will travel during the time that elapses from the fall of the hammer to the arrival of the various sizes of shot at the distances named :—

TABLE OF ALLOWANCES FOR AIMING AT A CROSSING BIRD.

Size of Shot.	Distance of Bird when the Hammer Falls.				
	20 yds.	25 yds.	30 yds.	35 yds.	40 yds.
3	3 ft. 8·0 in.	4 ft. 7·4 in.	5 ft. 9·6 in.	6 ft. 11·7 in.	8 ft. 2·6 in.
4	3 „ 8·0 „	4 „ 8·6 „	5 „ 10·2 „	7 „ 0·7 „	8 „ 4·1 „
5	3 „ 8·0 „	4 „ 8·7 „	5 „ 10·5 „	7 „ 1·2 „	8 „ 4·9 „
5½	3 „ 8·0 „	4 „ 8·8 „	5 „ 10·7 „	7 „ 1·6 „	8 „ 5·6 „
6	3 „ 8·0 „	4 „ 8·9 „	5 „ 10·9 „	7 „ 2·0 „	8 „ 6·1 „
6½	3 „ 8·0 „	4 „ 9·0 „	5 „ 11·1 „	7 „ 2·4 „	8 „ 6·7 „
7	3 „ 8·0 „	4 „ 9·1 „	5 „ 11·4 „	7 „ 2·8 „	8 „ 7·3 „

Here we have in an absolutely tangible form an important portion of the lesson that is to be learnt. . . . We find that in shooting at 20 yards the same allowance is required for all sizes of shot, the amount being 3 ft. 8 in., which is thus far greater than many would suppose. At 25 yards the required allowance is increased by practically another foot. At 30 yards there is a rather greater proportional increase, while at 35 yards the allowance becomes the very substantial one of 7 ft. or more. At 40 yards the shooter who desires to centre his charge of shot on a fast-flying bird travelling at right angles to the line of flight must aim rather more than 8 ft. in front of it.

Turning now to the differences in the specified allowances for the extreme sizes of shot shown in the table, it will be seen that up to 30 yards they are less than 2 in. At 35 yards the separation of values becomes more pronounced, and the difference is, practically speaking, 3 in., while at

40 yards it attains a maximum of just under 5 in. These figures entirely disprove the assumption that the shooter requires to alter his allowance when aiming at moving objects according to the size of shot in his gun. Adopting No. 6 shot as a standard size, we find that there is a difference of only 2 in. in the allowance for a 40-yard shot when a change is made to size No. 4. In view of the impossibility of knowing the precise velocity of the cartridge, the true range of the bird, and its correct rate of flight, it is obvious that such fractional differences as are created by a change in the size of shot are too infinitesimal for serious consideration. We accordingly adopt the allowance shown for size No. 6, and draw up the following exceedingly simple code of instructions to the shooter who desires to have a tangible idea of the allowance he must give to a fast-flying bird :—

When the bird is at 20 yards the shooter must allow	3 ft.	8 in.
,, ,, 25 ,, ,, ,,	4 ft.	9 in.
,, ,, 30 ,, ,, ,,	5 ft.	11 in.
,, ,, 35 ,, ,, ,,	7 ft.	2 in.
, ,, 40 ,, ,, ,.	8 ft.	6 in.

As already stated, the above allowances only represent the daylight between the bird and the point at which aim should be taken in the case of crossing shots. When a bird's flight is inclined so as to produce a foreshortening effect of its line of travel, the distance it covers is still the same, but the amount of daylight between the bird and the point at which aim is taken is a reducing quantity, which culminates at the zero mark when the bird is flying either directly towards or directly away from the shooter. This question of angle is, however, one which the shooter must instinctively settle for himself. If he knows approximately that the bird will move, say, 7 ft., while the shot is reaching it, he must decide in his own mind, according to the angle at which the bird is flying, whether this must represent 1 ft., 2 ft., or 3 ft., as the case may be, of daylight between the bird and the point aimed at."*

The investigations of the *Field* have thus shown, in a clear, accurate and definite form, the average amount of allowance that ought to be given for game flying at average speed at various distances. Further, it is demonstrated that, beyond perhaps a recognition that with small shot it is advisable to lead a trifle

* From the references to taking aim and not to swinging, it will be obvious that the *Field* is dealing only with the " mechanical " allowance.

more amply, no account need be taken, in this connection, of shot sizes. The precise methods to be adopted in translating theory into practice can be discovered only by individual experience. Each bird fired at goes at its own speed, whether 40 miles an hour, or more, or less, does not matter, since, whatever it may be, the bird sets the pace to the gun. What does matter, and matter profoundly, is that as the distance increases the movement of the gun is slowed. The method of shooting with a swinging gun, which is now being practised more and more generally, requires for its successful adoption a full realisation of the fact that in whatever way it may be done, this "slowing" on distant birds must be counteracted, of set purpose, if enough lead is to be given to the nearer, as distinguished from the more distant, birds. The apparent size of the object, with instantaneous recognition of its relation to surroundings such as trees, provides a clue to distance. Place 4-ft. and 8-ft. planks at measured distances of 20 yards and 40 yards against various backgrounds to accustom yourself to judge correct distance and allowance. The moving gun, quite irrespective of any consideration of measurements, is an actual indication of speed. The idea of the gun brought up to, swinging with, and passing the bird, may seem unavoidably to suggest the bad practice of " following." Nothing of the sort is really implied, for with all good shots who adopt this method the movement is nearly instantaneous, the gun going off practically as it gets to the shoulder. The further the bird is away, the greater will be the effect of muzzle movement in front of the mark, but the greater also the difficulty of accelerating that movement sufficiently, over and above the speed of gun set by the flight of the bird. The angular allowance on the moving gun barrel operates on the same principle as the rifleman's scale for windgauging, the muzzle movement producing an effect

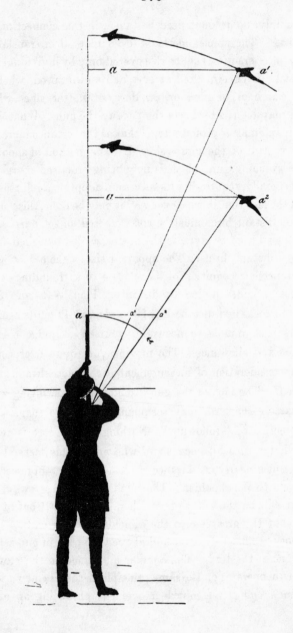

increasing as the range increases. Indeed, the homely analogy
of the cart-wheel shows at once that this must be so, for a spoke
revolving slowly at the hub covers ever-widening spaces, in
equal times, as its length is increased.

The simile of a cart-wheel has the advantage of suggesting
an easily comprehensible explanation why it is that high
birds seem to be slower than they really are, while low birds seem
faster than they really are. Imagine two pheasants both crossing
at the same speed, one fifteen yards high, and the other, quite a
tall bird, at thirty yards. Taking the gun as the hub end of the
spoke of a wheel, it is readily realized that a slow movement of
the barrel will suffice to keep the tall bird covered, for a wheel
with spokes thirty yards long would get over a great amount of
ground at each revolution. Turning, perhaps for the second
barrel, to the lower bird flying at half the height and going at the
same speed, the gun must move twice as fast to keep the bird
covered, because the spoke is only half the length. In like
manner, when shots are taken at really low birds, as in the
case of partridges driven over a hedge, the speed of gun movement may seem to be terrific, not because the partridge goes
any faster than the tall pheasant, but because he is so much
nearer the gun—or to keep up the simile because the partridge
is flying along the periphery of a little wheel with its spokes
moving fast.

Turning now to the silhouette illustration, it will be seen that
on the top line the distance from a^1 to a is exactly the same as
the distance from a^2 to a on the line below it. To preserve the
wheel simile, the two pheasants are shown flying in curves
forming segments of circles, but if they were crossing straight, and
both flying at the same rate, it is clear that the distance from a
to a^1 or a^2, would be flown in exactly equal times. The swinging
gun covers the birds and races ahead, but the travel of the gun

muzzle from a^2 to a is appreciably longer than the travel from a^1 to a, the swing being, of course, in the direction indicated by the arrow. As the time for both is equal, it follows that for the lower bird the gun must be moved much faster than for the upper bird.

According to this reasoning, high birds ought to be easier to align upon than low birds. So they are, but they are harder to hit. In the first place, if the shot is fired from a swinging gun without stopping the swing as the trigger is pulled, then a gun moving fast should more easily race ahead of the bird than a gun moving slowly would do. All this increases the likelihood of more lead being given for a near bird than the shooter fully realizes. On precisely the same grounds the high, and apparently slower, bird is apt to get less, because gun movement really is slower. There is no difficulty at all in realizing that if shot in one case has to go twice as far as it has in another case that alone will rather more than double the allowance ahead. Shot in flight loses its speed, and the smaller the size of pellet the more rapidly does velocity decrease.

PHRASEOLOGY.

The following terms were used in the past and are sometimes used still.

A nye of pheasants (a brood) ; *a paddling of duck* (a gathering); *a team of duck* (in flight) ; *a fall of woodcock* (a flock); *a skulk of foxes* (a troop) ; *a cete of badgers* (a company) ; *a sounder of swine* (a herd) ; *a singular of boars* (a pack) ; *a pride of lions* (a group) ; *a sege of herons* (a flock) ; *a herd of swans* (a large number of swans feeding or travelling together) ; *a spring of teal* (a flock) ; *a covert of coots* (a flock) ; *a gaggle of geese* (a flock of geese on the water) ; *a skein of geese* (a flock in flight) ; *a sord or sute of mallard* (a flock) ; *a company of widgeon, a trip of wildfowl* (a collection of waterfowl) ; *a rush or flight of pollard, a dopping of sheldrakes, a bevy of quails* (a flock) ; *a covey of partridges or grouse* (a flock) ; *a pack of grouse* (a gathering of coveys) ; a *congregation of plovers* (a flock) ; *a walk of snipe* (a flock) ; *a wisp of snipe* (a flight) ; *a building of rooks* (a company or rookery) ; *a murmuration of starlings* (a flock) : *a cast of hawks, a sleuth of bears, a gang of elk.*

WEIGHTS OF GAME.

Blackcock	... 3 lbs. to 4 lbs	Ptarmigan	... 1 lb. to 1½ lbs.
Capercailzie	... 6 lbs. to 12 lbs.	Quail	... 3 ozs. to 4 ozs.
Golden Plover	... 7 ozs. to 9 ozs.	Rabbit	... 2½lbs. to 3½ lbs.
Grouse	... 1 lb. to 1¾ lbs.	Snipe, common	... 3½ ozs. to 4½ ozs.
Hare	... 6½ lbs. to 7 lbs.	Snipe, jack	... 1½ ozs. to 2½ ozs.
Mallard	... 2 lbs. to 3 lbs.	Widgeon	... 1¼ lbs. to 2 lbs.
Partridge	... 13 ozs. to 15 ozs.	Woodcock	... 8 ozs. to 14 ozs.
Pheasant	... 2½ lbs. to 3½ lbs.	Woodpigeon	... 1 lb. to 1¼ lbs.

The above weights are those usually attained to by ordinary well-grown specimens, but it must not be forgotten that occasionally exceptional weights are recorded, much exceeding those given.

Charles Lancaster.

In 1826 Charles Lancaster founded, at 151, New Bond Street, what soon became the world-famous gun-making business bearing his name. He had previously attained great eminence as a barrel maker and supplied the barrels used by Joe Manton and other celebrated gunmakers. Colonel Hawker, the great sportsman of that period, wrote of him in his well-known book on shooting as follows :—

" Lancaster, who has raised many gunmakers to the head of the trade by allowing them to put their names to what was his work in all the essential parts of the barrels, has long since started for himself. This I advised him to do if ever Joe Manton retired . . . I may safely say that no man stands before him."

This opinion must have been shared by many other sportsmen, for Charles Lancaster at once became one of the great and fashionable gunmakers. His rise to fame was not only immediate but progressive and over seventy First Class Prizes, Medals and Diplomas were awarded to him.

The " Twelve-Twenty " gun was probably the firm's most outstanding model and it alone would have been sufficient to make the name of Charles Lancaster one of the most famous in the history of gunmaking.

Henry Atkin, Ltd.

Established in 1862 this firm traded for 60 years in Jermyn Street, and subsequently at 27, St. James's Street until 1960, when it amalgamated with Grant & Lang to form the present company. Its guns were of the highest quality and the spring-opening model is widely admired.

Stephen Grant & Sons.

Stephen Grant—a man of great experience and exceptional skill in the building of best quality guns and rifles—commenced business on his own account at 67A, St. James's Street in 1866 and from the very first he occupied a prominent position in the front rank of famous London gunmakers.

With a clientele desiring only the very finest guns and rifles that skill and money could produce, Mr. Grant naturally devoted his whole attention to the production of best quality weapons. After being carried on for nine decades that tradition has now become like the laws of the Medes and Persians.

Joseph Lang & Son.

In 1821 Joseph Lang commenced for himself by acquiring an old-established business, which he developed into a great and world-wide connection. The policy he adopted was to produce guns and rifles of the highest standard of design, workmanship and finish, and even secondhand weapons were not offered for sale in his establishment unless they had been made by the most eminent London makers of that period. In the "Morning Chronicle" of the 8th June, 1826, he advertised the entire stock of Joe Manton.

At a later period, to meet the requirements of those who for various reasons did not wish to purchase the most expensive guns, he introduced several cheaper models which were greatly appreciated and enabled every sportsman to obtain the best value for whatever price he wished to pay.

In opening his Shooting Range in 1827 he was the pioneer of the modern Shooting School. In 1852 he introduced the breech-loading gun into England and many inventions and improvements will always be associated with his name.

Harrison & Hussey.

After the end of the Great War this firm was commenced by bearers of these names, both of whom died within ten years. A wonderful connection had been built up in such a short time, but as it was decided not to continue the business, we acquired it in 1930.

Watson Bros.

This firm was founded in 1875, by acquiring the business and premises of Durs Egg, one of the great names in gun-making, who had also achieved world renown as a pistol maker as early as 1785.

They carried on business for 60 years as Old Bond Street and Pall Mall till purchased by Grant & Lang Ltd. in 1935. Besides a very fine general connection, they made a speciality of small bore guns for ladies and boys.

In 1984 Watson Bros. was purchased and incorporated in the firm Hellis, Beesely & Watson.

F. Beesley.

This business was established in 1880 and was carried on by the founder and his son at 2, St. James's Street, till purchased by Grant & Lang Ltd. in 1939. Mr. Beesley was a man of great skill and some even of his earlier inventions are still considered amongst the best. Catering principally for the highest class of trade, he had built up an extremely fine connection.

In 1984 F. Beesley was acquired from Churchill, Atkin, Grant & Lang and is now incorporated in Hellis, Beesley & Watson.

Charles Hellis & Sons.

Commenced in 1894, this business was carried on in Edgware Road by the founder and two following generations until acquired by Henry Atkin in 1956. Although many Hellis guns were made, the firm was probably best known for its extensive trade in cartridges.

In 1984 the proprietors of Churchill, Atkin, Grant & Lang sold Charles Hellis & Sons (who made over 5,000 guns) and it was incorporated into Hellis, Beesley & Watson.

"The Workmanship is Faultless"

Quote on the Dickson 'Round-Action' gun from The Modern Shotgun (1931).

"Nothing has changed"

Quote on the new availability of the same gun from John Dickson (1983).

We are pleased to announce that our famous Patent 'Round-Action' hammerless ejector gun is once again available to order.

We also offer an extremely comprehensive range of new and used guns and rifles, clothing and accessories at our four branches.

John Dickson & Son

GUN, RIFLE AND FISHING TACKLE MAKERS. ESTAB. 1820
21 Frederick Street, Edinburgh Tel: 031-225 4218.

20 Exchange Square, Glasgow.
Tel: 041-221 6794.

35 Belmont Street, Aberdeen.
Tel: Aberdeen 640480.

35 Square, Kelso.
Tel: Kelso 324687.

185

S. R. Jeffery & Son Ltd.

134 High Street, Guildford

Established Over 125 Years
Quality Guns Rifles & Ammunition
Clothing & Accessories.

0483 – 505055

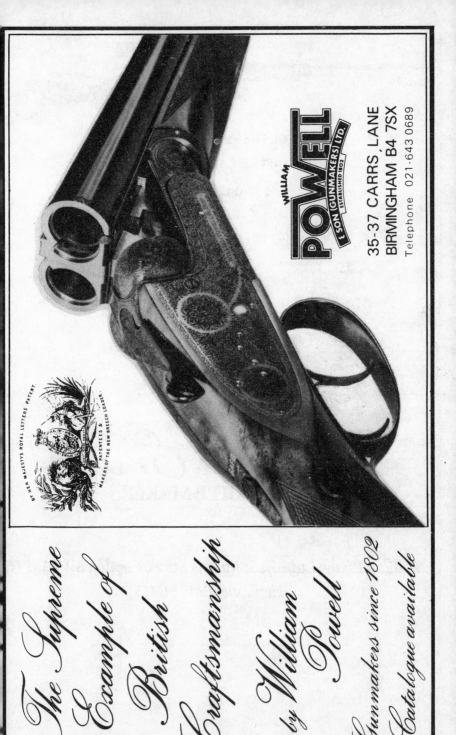
189

The following pages are devoted to the inclusion of advertisments taken from previous editions and are therefore long out of date. The passing of the years has bestowed upon them sufficient charms of nostalgia to merit their reappearance here.

WHATEVER THE GAME

See that
your
CARTRIDGES
have
a head like this

● Whether you buy proprietary branded cartridges, or ammunition loaded by your own gunmaker, you are safe in your selection if the heads have the ELEY-KYNOCH mark.

It is a guarantee of quality; all cases, powder, and wads being matched to ensure perfect balance and complete reliability.

 Buy British Ammunition.

IMPERIAL CHEMICAL INDUSTRIES LIMITED, MILLBANK, LONDON, S.W.1

PRESENTATION GUNS

We specialise in weapons specially suitable for presentation purposes. The elaborate engraving and gold inlaying are carried out by our own workmen and as applied to a best gun or rifle represent the highest standard of modern gunmaking. Special designs prepared to customer's own suggestions.

ESTIMATES FREE.

JOSEPH LANG & SON'S SIDE-LOCK GUNS

Second Quality - £90

Third Quality - £70

JOSEPH LANG & SON'S

Box-Lock Guns

Best Quality - £52 10 0

Second Quality - £36 15 0

Worthy of special mention as being ideal for ladies or elderly gentlemen is the 12-bore gun which weighs only 5¼ lbs. and fires a two-inch cartridge with remarkable results. Built in all above qualities.

Patent single trigger mechanism, £10 10s. extra in all above qualities.

Plain Quality Box-Lock - £26 5 0

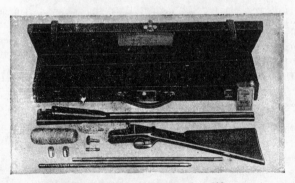

BOYS' GUNS, 28 bore and ·410

Double Barrel Ejector	-	£19 19 0	complete in case
Non-ejector	-	-	15 15 0	complete in case
·410 Single Barrel		4 4 0	(no case)

GRANT & LANG
SPECIAL CARTRIDGES

With our special "Velogrant" load only. (A charge of selected powder and size of shot designed to give increased velocity with best all-round results.)

Loaded with a good smokeless powder, this is an excellent cartridge for rabbit, vermin or clay bird shooting.

"EJECTOR," Indian red paper, covered 2¼in. brass, metal lined.
"PEGAMOID," waterproof ⅜in. brass, metal lined.
"GRANTBURY," water-resisting, ⅜in. brass, metal lined.
"ROCKETER," ⅜in. brass, unlined.
"INSTANTER," $\frac{5}{16}$in. brass, unlined.

These are all steadily growing in favour, and each quality represents a standard of excellence that cannot be surpassed. They are carefully loaded to order with "Smokeless Diamond," "E.C.," "Empire," "Schultze" or "Amberite" powder and any size of shot.

Our Cartridge Department is organized to ensure accurate loading and prompt despatch.

Special Cartridge Price List post free on application

Small bores and all rifle cartridges supplied at short notice.

GRANT & LANG'S
Shooting Grounds

LARGE AND LAVISHLY EQUIPPED

The best and most up-to-date Grounds for
Practice and Instruction in all kinds of Shooting

WALKING-UP-GAME from carefully
concealed traps behind natural cover

RABBIT SHOOTING - - -

GROUSE DRIVING FROM BUTTS

PARTRIDGE DRIVING OVER HEDGES

PHEASANT SHOOTING over tall
trees, also from towers with stages
at various heights up to 120 feet

Gun fitting with "try-guns" a speciality.
Guns by any maker can be used.

TERMS AND APPOINTMENTS ON APPLICATION

HIGH VELOCITY
DOUBLE-BARRELLED RIFLES

In Bores from ·256 to ·600 and rifled on the grooved system, giving extreme accuracy and great stopping power.

Of special interest is the celebrated Lancaster ·280, which with 24½ in. barrels weighs 9½ lbs., handles like a shot gun and is an ideal weapon for stalking at home and abroad, £140.

Plainer Quality Rifles at £95 and £70.

Magazine Rifles in calibres from ·22 to ·404 at current prices

NOTE.—All particulars and prices are subject to alteration without notice. As many customers who buy a gun do not require a gun-case or preliminary fitting at the Shooting Grounds, the price of a weapon does not include these items.

TERMS.—All prices quoted are for prompt net cash and 10% extra is charged on overdue accounts.

FULLY ILLUSTRATED CATALOGUE FREE ON APPLICATION

BURBERRY
GABARDINE
SUITS

To the man who studies to make himself invisible to game there are several shades so perfect in this respect in Burberry Gabardines and one in particular which a well-known game shot gave up wearing because it was so inconspicuous he feared it might be overlooked by his next guns.

In addition to invisibility an equally important item in shooting is to have a coat in which the set of a gun will be perfect and that without the slightest restriction to arm freedom, and for this the Burberry Gabardine shooting coat is so excellent.

Illustrations, patterns and prices sent on mention of " The Art of Shooting."

BURBERRYS LTD.
HAYMARKET, LONDON, S.W.I

THE BURBERRY

The World's Best Weatherproof

The Burberry is the sportsman's ideal top-coat. Warm
without weight, proof without heat, self-ventilating and
therefore healthful, it enables
one to shoot quickly and
accurately.

The loose construction of
The Burberry at the shoulder
allows perfect freedom for
quick shooting. With the
Burberry, a spell on the
moors gives maximum satisfaction—let the weather be
what it may.

*Illustrations, patterns and prices sent on
mention of "The Art of Shooting."*

BURBERRYS

HAYMARKET
LTD. LONDON, S.W.I

200

201

STEPHEN GRANT & SONS'
Best Quality Side-Lock Hammerless Ejector Guns

Since Stephen Grant started business seventy years ago, his name on a gun has always been a sign of the highest quality. It is our constant endeavour not only to keep to this ideal but by improvements in design to present to sportsmen those refinements which are also reliable and useful.

Top Lever.

The most important recent development is the production of an easy-opening action which also has the great advantage of being easy to close both before and after firing. The sales of this gun are clear evidence of its well-deserved popularity.

Side Lever.

Top or Side Lever - £110
Self-Opening Models £120

Too good to miss . . .

Authoritative articles on all aspects of shooting appear regularly in *The Field*. Be sure you don't miss this week's copy.

JOSEPH LANG & SON'S

" Under and Over " Gun.

Highest Quality only.

Double Trigger or fitted with the Lang Single Trigger (as illustrated).

F. BEESLEY gave special attention to 16 bores, best quality sidelock as illustrated above, and in the qualities shown on pages 196 and 197.

WATSON BROS.' small bore guns, in all qualities.

HARRISON & HUSSEY guns can be built to match existing ones.

FLINTWEAR use GANNEX cloth in this practical shooting coat.

Completely waterproof, completely windproof, prevents condensation, stain repellent, easily cleaned and extremely hard wearing.

FLINTWEAR clothing was used on all Everest Expeditions from 1933 to the final success under Sir John Hunt in 1953.

It has also been used on innumerable other expeditions, by British Olympic Ski and Yacht Teams and by famous sportsmen everywhere.

HOWARD FLINT LTD.
18 Grosvenor Street, London, W.1
May 3282

207

WHEN IN LONDON a visit to Milwards Shop in Bury Street is well worthwhile.

Our experienced and keen staff will be glad to show you any item from our range of first class, modern design fishing tackle, and to answer any questions about these, or any other subject to do with angling.

Similarly enquiries by post or telephone will have prompt and interested attention.

MILWARDS
FISHING TACKLE LIMITED
(H. MILWARD & SONS—Established 1730)

**7 BURY STREET, ST. JAMES'S,
LONDON, S.W.1**
Telephone: WHItehall 0151/4